The Vegetarian Ch
of Britain

The Vegetarian Chefs of Britain

*A wonderful collection of recipes
from many of the leading vegetarian chefs
of Great Britain*

ABSOLUTE PRESS

First published in 1993 by Absolute Press
Scarborough House, 29 James Street West, Bath, England

© Absolute Press 1996
This edition first published November 1996

Editor: Nicki Morris

Cover and illustrations: Caroline Nisbett
Design: Ian Middleton

Printed by Longdunn Press Ltd, Bristol.

ISBN 0 948230 82 7

Contents

Introduction

Down with cheese omelettes! The days of the vegetarian as second-class citizen are long gone and restaurants can no longer get away with offering nothing more than a collection of wilting side-dish vegetables or the ubiquitous omelette to their vegetarian customers; indeed they are often judged on the quality of the vegetarian alternatives featured on their menus. The new status of vegetarian food is reflected in this collection of recipes from some of the most innovative vegetarian chefs cooking in Britain today. From the small, intimate bistro to the vegetarian country house hotel, a recurring theme emerges: the desire to provide a comfortable, pleasurable dining experience that vegetarians can enjoy along with the rest of the restaurant-going public. Perhaps the most telling advertisement for the recipes comes from the many chefs who have commented on the fact that the vegetarian dishes they offer are often chosen by staunch meat-eaters as an experiment – and that they often come back for a return visit!

Editor's note

The Vegetarian Chefs of Britain was first published in 1993. Since that time some of the restaurants featured have either closed down, changed hands or taken on different chefs.

Yolanda Bloor

ex-DYLANS RESTAURANT · HANLEY

With help from the Prince's Youth Business Trust, British Coal Enterprises, plus friends and relatives, Dylans was opened on a shoestring in April 1988. Since then, the restaurant has made steady progress, establishing a good reputation and a large clientele. It has since changed hands but continues to provide a relaxed setting with old-fashioned decor, low lighting and unobtrusive music, in which to enjoy tasty vegetarian and vegan meals at good value for money.

CREAM CHEESE AND CHIVE DIP

Serves 4

*2 x 7 oz (200g) packets cream cheese
juice of ¹/₂ lemon
bunch fresh chives, finely chopped
¹/₂ small carton cream
salt and pepper to taste
few extra chives and ¹/₂ teaspoon paprika to garnish*

Mix together the cream cheese, lemon juice, cream and chives. Mix well, then add salt and pepper to taste.

Sprinkle the remaining chives and paprika over the top and serve with a garnish of different coloured lettuce leaves and a selection of tortilla chips.

MUSHROOM AND WALNUT STRUDEL

Serves 4

*2 large cloves garlic
2 large onions, peeled and sliced
1 lb (450g) washed, sliced mushrooms
2 tablespoons fresh or 4 tablespoons dried parsley
vegetable oil
4 oz (125g) roughly chopped walnuts
8 fl oz (225ml) red wine
1 pint (570ml) vegetable stock
salt and pepper to taste
1 packet filo pastry
4 oz (125g) melted butter*

Fry the garlic, onions, mushrooms and parsley until soft. Add the walnuts, wine and stock and simmer gently for about 10 minutes or until the mixture is cooked through. Taste and season the mixture. Strain the vegetables out of the mixture and save the gravy.

Grease an ovenproof dish with some of the melted butter and place 3-4 layers of filo on the bottom of the dish, brushing each layer with melted butter. Place half the vegetable and nut mixture over the layer of pastry, followed by another 3-4 layers of filo, again brushing each layer with melted butter.

Make the next layer with the remainder of the vegetable and nut mixture and finish off with at least 4-5 layers of filo pastry and melted butter. Brush all over the top with melted butter and bake in a medium oven until golden.

Serve the strudel with the reserved gravy (it can be thickened with a little cornflour if needed). New potatoes and a green salad make an ideal accompaniment.

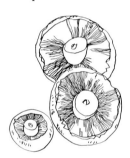

PASSION FRUIT MOUSSE

Serves 4-6

1 tin condensed milk
1 pint (570ml) fresh cream, stiffly whipped
8 passion fruit

First caramelise the condensed milk by placing the tin in a pan of water - bring the water to the boil and cook for $1\frac{1}{2}$ hours. Make sure the tin remains totally immersed in the boiling water - on no account let it boil dry.

Let the condensed milk cool, then gently stir it into the whipped cream. Vary the amount of condensed milk depending on how sweet you want the mousse – I use about $\frac{1}{2}$ tin to 1 pint (570ml) cream.

Next scoop out the insides of the passion fruit, add to the cream mixture and mix well. Place the mixture in serving dishes and chill in the refrigerator. When ready to serve, decorate with fruit, chopped nuts or grated chocolate.

Brian Bunce

A huge range of vegetarian starters and main courses is offered at the Druid Inn, a beautiful ivy-clad building set in the rural village of Birchover, in the Peak Park. A comfortable ambience in which to enjoy your meal, whether meat-eater or vegetarian, is the order of the day, with fires burning during the winter months and even on cold and damp days in the summer!

TARKA DHAL

Serves 4

4 oz (125g) red split lentils
1/2 large onion, diced
pinch salt
1/2 teaspoon ground turmeric
1/2 teaspoon ground cumin
1/2 teaspoon ground coriander
2 bay leaves
2 pints (1.1 litres)
4 small potatoes, peeled and quartered
4 tablespoons oil mixed with 2 tablespoons clarified butter
3 cloves garlic, thinly sliced
1 small onion, thinly sliced

naan bread or puppadoms, to serve

Place the lentils, diced onion, salt, spices and water in a pan; bring to the boil and allow to simmer for approx. 40 minutes until the lentils are pureed. Add the potatoes halfway through the cooking time.

Heat the butter and oil in a separate pan and fry the garlic and sliced onion gently until golden brown. Slowly add the lentil purée to the garlic and onion and simmer for a few minutes until it has browned slightly.

Serve with either naan bread or puppadoms.

KASHMIRI PILAFF

Serves 4

1 cup oil
1 small onion, diced
2 teaspoons chopped fresh garlic
1 teaspoon chopped fresh root ginger
6 whole black peppercorns
6 green cardamom pods
4 whole cloves
4 bay leaves
1 pint (570ml) cold water
1 lb (500g) basmati rice, rinsed in cold water
4 oz (125g) dried apricots, dried
4 oz (125g) walnuts, halved
2 oz (50g) sultanas

2 tablespoons oil
1/4 small onion, finely diced
1 jar smooth peanut butter
pinch coriander
salt and pepper to taste
3 cups cold water
1 tablespoon clear honey
1 tablespoon lemon juice

Heat the oil in a pan and add the onion, garlic, ginger and spices. Cook until lightly browned. Add the water and bring to the boil.

Add the rice, cover the pan with a tight-fitting lid and simmer on a low heat until the rice is half cooked. Add the apricots, walnuts and sultanas and leave on a low heat until the rice is cooked.

To make the sauce, heat the oil and sweat off the onions, turn to a low heat and add the peanut butter, stirring continuously. Add the coriander, salt and pepper, then slowly add the water. Add the honey and lemon juice, stirring slowly and allow to reduce to the required consistency, without allowing to boil. Allow to cool and liquidise.

Serve the rice with the sauce poured over, with a crisp green salad, dressed with a honey and oil dressing.

APPLE AND MARZIPAN TORTE

Serves 6

rich shortcrust pastry to line a 10 inch (25cm)
baking tin
4 oz (125g) demerara sugar
4 oz (125g) margarine
2 egg whites
4 oz (125g) grated apple
4 oz (125g) grated marzipan

Line the baking tin with the pastry. Cream the margarine and sugar and add the stiffly whisked egg whites. Fold in the grated apple and marzipan and pour into the pastry case.

Using pastry remnants, form a criss-cross design over the filling. Bake at 400F/200C/Gas 6, reducing the temperature slightly after 35 minutes.

David Burton

Hockneys is run in accordance with Buddhist ideals and ethical principles by men associated with the 'Friends of the Western Buddhist Order'. We endeavour to provide a meaningful livelihood for ourselves, a useful service to the community, and nutritious, tasty food which causes no harm to animals.

PUMPKIN SOUP

Serves 4-6

1 lb (450g) onions, chopped
vegetable oil
1 clove garlic, chopped
2 lbs (900g) pumpkin flesh, chopped
1 large carrot, diced
1 large potato, diced
1 dessertspoon ground coriander
1/2 dessertspoon powdered ginger
7 oz (200g) coconut cream
salt and pepper
pinch brown sugar
vegetable bouillon cube (optional)

Fry the onions in vegetable oil with the garlic until soft. Add the pumpkin flesh, carrot, potato, coriander and ginger. Top up with water to make 2 pints (1.1 litres). Do not add too much water as the soup should be quite thick. Bring to the boil and cook until the vegetables are soft.

Add the chopped coconut cream and turn off the heat. Liquidise until smooth. Season with salt, pepper, a pinch of brown sugar and a vegetable bouillon cube (optional).

PEACOCK PIE

Serves 6

FOR THE FILLING:
6 oz (175g) blackeye beans
1 oz (25g) white mustard seeds
vegetable oil
4 oz (125g) cashew nuts
1½ lbs (700g) onions, chopped
10 oz (275g) coconut cream
1/4 bunch dill
1/4 bunch coriander leaves
salt, pepper and lemon juice

FOR THE TOPPING:
1 lb (450g) cauliflower
2 oz (50g) butter, melted
1½ lbs (700g) tinned tomatoes
4 oz (125g) Cheddar cheese, grated
salt and white pepper

Boil the blackeye beans until quite soft. 'Pop' the mustard seeds in oil, being careful not to burn them. Add the cashew nuts and fry for 2 minutes. Add the onion and cook until soft without colouring, again being careful not to burn. Drain this mixture.

Melt the coconut cream over a very low heat. It must not go brown but should remain pure white. Combine the drained onion mixture, drained blackeye beans, finely chopped dill and coriander, melted coconut cream, salt, pepper and a little lemon juice.

To make the topping, boil the cauliflower until soft and drain well. Add the melted butter, the well-drained and chopped tinned tomatoes, grated Cheddar, salt and white pepper. Liquidise very well until completely smooth.

Place the filling in a 9 x 5 inch (23 x 12.5cm) baking tin and smooth the top. Add the topping and shake the tin gently until smooth. Bake in the oven at 375F/190C/Gas 5 for about 45 minutes.

FRUITY CASHEW CAKE

Makes about 16 pieces

1¹/₂ lbs (700g) dried dates

6 oz (175g) cashew nuts
11 oz (300g) raisins
6 oz (175g) desiccated coconut
6 oz (175g) rolled oats
7 oz (200g) wholewheat flour
1 dessertspoon baking powder

4¹/₂ lbs (2.1kg) mushy bananas
11 fl oz (300ml) vegetable oil
¹/₂ teaspoon salt
1 teaspoon vanilla essence

Boil the dates with 3/4 pint (400ml) water for about 10 minutes until fairly smooth. Leave to cool.

Combine the dry ingredients together and liquidise the bananas with the oil, salt and vanilla essence. Add the wet mix to the dry and combine thoroughly.

Line a deep 11 x 9 inch (28 x 23cm) baking tin with greaseproof paper. Spread half of the cake mix over the bottom of the tin. Spread the date mixture over this layer. Spread the remaining half of the cake mix on top and cover with greaseproof paper. Bake at 350F/180C/Gas 4 for about 70 minutes.

Tessa Bramley

THE OLD VICARAGE · RIDGEWAY MOOR

*The emphasis at the Old Vicarage is on innovative, exciting food which retains its
roots in the unpretentious, honest tradition of country cooking; this applies to the
vegetarian dishes as well as everything else on the menu. The most important factor
in Tessa Bramley's vegetarian cooking is the selection of the very best vegetables in
season when they are at their most flavoursome. Equally important is the use of
good oils for cooking and dressings; fine vinegars make a world of difference too.
Fresh herbs are also absolutely indispensable – grow them on the windowsill from
seed if you have difficulty buying what you need.*

LEEK AND MUSHROOM CANNELLONI WITH TOMATO CROSTINI

Serves 4

5 oz (150g) plain flour
1/2 teaspoon salt
1 tablespoon water infused with pinch saffron
stamens
1 egg
1 dessertspoon olive oil

FOR THE FILLING:
2 leeks, finely chopped
8 mushrooms, chopped
2 tablespoons extra virgin olive oil
3 sprigs thyme
scraping of nutmeg
1 oz (25g) pine kernels, toasted until golden

FOR THE SAUCE:
15 fl oz (400ml) double cream
thyme leaves
seasoning
1 oz (25g) grated Gruyère or Parmesan
1 loaf stale ciabatta (Italian olive oil bread)
1 clove garlic
extra virgin olive oil
good flavoured tomatoes
spring onions, chopped
basil leaves, shredded
balsamic vinegar

To make the pasta, add the liquid ingredients
to the dry in a processor until the mixture
holds together. Turn out and knead until shiny
and smooth. Wrap and chill for 1 hour. Roll out
on a floured surface into thin lengths (or using
No 6 gauge on a pasta machine). Cut into
pieces approx. 4 inches x 3 inches (10cm x
7.5cm). Moisten one edge and fold over to
make a tube. Dry out on a broom handle for
about 1 hour. When dry cook in boiling salted

water for 2-3 minutes. Rinse well and pat dry.

Fry the prepared vegetables in olive oil until softened. Add the thyme leaves, pine kernels and seasonings. Fill the tubes with the leek filling and arrange in an ovenproof dish.

Reduce the cream with the thyme leaves until thickened slightly. Season. Pour over the cannelloni and sprinkle with the cheese. Bake in a hot oven (425F/220C/Gas 7) for about 5 minutes until golden.

Cut 4 thickish slices of ciabatta, rub them with a cut clove of garlic and drizzle with olive oil. Dry out in the oven until crusty. Slice the tomatoes and sprinkle with the spring onions and basil. Make a salad dressing with the vinegar and olive oil and seasoning and pour over the tomatoes (I like to drop 2 or 3 cloves of garlic into the dressing jar to allow the flavour to infuse.)

Remove the cannelloni and crostini from the oven. Sit the tomato salad on the crostini and serve alongside the cannelloni with a little of the cream sauce poured round.

AUBERGINE AND SQUASH SATAY WITH CARROT, GINGER AND LIME FILOS AND CHILLI AND SESAME POTATO CAKES

Serves 4

4 thick slices aubergine, cut into cubes
1 butternut squash, cut into thick cubes
16 button mushrooms
2 teaspoons five spices
2 tablespoons olive oil
1 red chilli, finely chopped
seasoning

FOR THE POTATO CAKES:
8 oz (225g) mashed potatoes, seasoned
6 green cardamom pods, seeds crushed
2 teaspoons chopped fresh coriander leaves
2 red chillis, seeds removed, very finely chopped
sesame seeds
sesame oil

FOR THE CARROT FILOS:
8 sheets filo pastry
1 1/2 lbs (700g) carrot purée
grated rind of 1 lime
1 piece stem ginger, cut into fine julienne strips
salt and freshly ground black pepper
pinch sugar, if needed

2 oz (50g) basmati rice, made into a dry risotto flavoured with fresh coriander leaves

satay dipping sauce, sweet and sour sauce, tomato sauce or concasse, to serve

Thread the aubergine and squash cubes with the mushrooms alternately on to 8 wooden satay sticks. Mix the spices, oil and seasoning, roll the skewers in this marinade and pour a little over them. Roast in a hot oven (425F/220C/Gas 7) for 5-6 minutes, turning in the marinade to keep moist.

Mix the first 4 ingredients for the potato cakes together. Taste and check for seasoning. Shape into 8 small potato cakes, roll in sesame seeds and chill. Fry in sesame oil (using a cast iron pan, very hot, if possible) until crusty and golden. Keep hot.

Lay 2 overlapping sheets of buttered filo on the work surface, with the bottom sheet at an angle, to form a star shape. Mix the carrot purée with the other ingredients and put 1 tablespoon of the purée in the centre of the filo. Gather up the sides to centre and twist to form a purse shape. Bake at 425F/220C/Gas 7 for about 10 minutes until golden.

To assemble the dish, sit 2 satay sticks per portion on to a bed of risotto. Place 1 teaspoon satay dipping sauce at the side. Place the carrot filo to one side of the satays and pour over a little sweet and sour sauce. Spoon a good tomato sauce (or concasse) on the other side and sit the potato cakes on it.

BRANDY SNAP BASKETS OF HONEY ICE CREAM WITH STRAWBERRY AND ROSEWATER COULIS

Serves 4

FOR THE BRANDY SNAPS:
4 tablespoons golden syrup
4 oz (125g) butter
4 oz (125g) dark brown sugar
4 oz (125g) plain flour
1 level teaspoon ground ginger
FOR THE HONEY ICE CREAM:
8 egg whites
6 oz (175g) icing sugar
1 pint (570ml) double cream
2 tablespoons wild flower honey
FOR THE COULIS:
1 lb (450g) strawberries
1 tablespoon rosewater
caster sugar to taste

Heat the syrup, butter and sugar in a pan until melted. Sieve together the flour and ginger, add to the mixture and beat until smooth. Put walnut-sized balls of the mixture on to a greased baking tray. Spread with your fingertips into circles and bake at 325F/160C/Gas 3 for 5-7 minutes.

Remove from the oven and settle for a minute or so. When possible, lift the biscuits from the tin , drape over a lemon or small pudding mould and squeeze into a tulip shape while still warm. Repeat to make 4 cups, leave to cool and remove from the moulds. Store in an airtight tin.

To make the ice cream, whisk the egg whites until stiff. Add the sugar, gradually whisking in to form a meringue. Whisk the cream and honey together until floppy. Fold the meringue into the cream, pour into a 2 litre ($3^{1}/_{2}$ pint) container and freeze until firm.

Purée the strawberries with the rosewater and caster sugar. Pass through a sieve. Scoop the ice cream into the brandy snap baskets and pour a little of the sauce around.

Dave Clement

We opened Clements three years ago with the idea of breaking away from the traditional concept of the vegetarian café/restaurant and creating an unashamedly up-market establishment - there seemed no reason why vegetarian food should not be elegantly presented in sophisticated surroundings. Our tables are attractively set with fine glasses, linen napkins, flowers and candles and the aim is to give customers a memorable evening out - to this end an extensive range of organic wines, including organic champagne is on offer. For us, vegetarian cooking offers much broader scope than classical traditional cooking and the scope for innovation is endless - we get great satisfaction from developing new dishes, combining different vegetables, nuts, herbs, pulses etc., to give a range of subtle textures and tastes.

BUTTERBEAN AND CORIANDER DIP WITH CRUDITES

Serves 6-8

2 x 15 oz (425g) tins butterbeans
2 cloves garlic
3½ fl oz (100ml) olive oil
3½ fl oz (100ml) lemon juice
few sprigs coriander
few sprigs parsley
½ teaspoon salt
pepper

FOR THE CRUDITES:
carrots, peppers, cucumber (sliced)
whole radishes
cauliflower florets
celery
crisps (optional)

Drain the butterbeans and place in a food processor. Peel the garlic and add to the processor. Add all the remaining ingredients and process well into a smooth paste. Taste and add more seasoning if required.

Wash and chop the vegetables. Arrange on a plate surrounding the pot of dip.

HAZELNUT ROAST EN CROUTE

Serves 4-5

8 oz (225g) wholemeal breadcrumbs
6 oz (175g) chopped hazelnuts
4 oz (125g) grated carrot
2 oz (50g) onion, chopped in processor
2 oz (50g) celery, chopped in processor
¼ teaspoon salt
pepper
1 small clove garlic, crushed

1 teaspoon mixed herbs
2 tablespoons oil
2 tablespoons tomato juice
5 sheets filo pastry
sunflower oil for brushing

Mix the first 9 ingredients together in a bowl. Add the oil and tomato juice and mix well. Form the mixture into 5 x 5 oz (150g) balls.

Oil the surface of the table or worktop well, using a pastry brush and sunflower oil. Place one of the sheets of filo pastry on to the oiled surface. Brush the filo with oil, fold the sheet in half, then oil the edges. Place a hazelnut ball in the centre of the filo, then carefully gather the pastry up to the top. Pinch the gathered filo together so that none of the filling is showing and the filo forms a neat purse with the edges overhanging.

Oil the outside of the parcel, place on a lined baking tray and complete the other 4 balls in the same way. Place a sheet of aluminium foil over the tray and cook in a preheated oven at 350F/180C/Gas 4 for 15 minutes. Then remove the foil and turn the tray around in the oven and cook for a further 10 minutes until crisp and golden. These en croûtes freeze well and should be cooked under foil for a further 15 minutes after defrosting.

TOFU CHEESECAKE

Serves 6-8

FOR THE BASE:
8 oz (225g) digestive biscuits
2 oz (50g) margarine

FOR THE TOPPING:
2 oz (50g) dates
2 tablespoons lemon juice
3 tablespoons water
1 packet firm silken tofu
1 large ripe banana
5 fl oz (150ml) apple juice
$^1/_2$ teaspoon vanilla essence
1 dessertspoon tahini

Crush the digestive biscuits in a mixing bowl. Melt the margarine and add to the digestive biscuits. Mix thoroughly then press into an 8 inch (20.5cm) round cake tin base.

Stew the dates in the lemon juice and water until the liquid evaporates. Mix all the remaining ingredients together and mix well with the dates in a mixing bowl. Spread over the base and smooth over the top.

Place in the oven at 350F/180C/Gas 4 for 40-45 minutes until golden brown and springy. Serve chilled topped with fresh fruit.

Elizabeth Cousins

Tiffins, Harrogate's only vegetarian restaurant, was opened in 1988. Although I have since had two children, I still play a very active part in the running of the restaurant, along with my hard-working staff. While meeting the needs of vegetarians and vegans, the majority of Tiffins' customers are meat-eaters and so the menu has also to appeal to the most sceptical omnivore. Our blackboard menu changes daily and is drawn from a wide range of cultures and cuisines. While we always use wholefood ingredients, Tiffins does not regard itself as a 'health food restaurant' - some dishes are fried and often laden with calories (like our highly regarded Sticky Toffee Pudding). Tiffins has been awarded a distinction in the Vegetarian Good Food Guide.

FRENCH ONION SOUP WITH HERB SCONES

Serves 4

FOR THE SOUP:
2-3 large onions, finely sliced
3 tablespoons oil
1½ pints (900ml) vegetable stock
2 teaspoons mixed herbs
1 teaspoon yeast extract
salt and pepper to taste

FOR THE SCONES:
8 oz (225g) wholemeal self-raising flour
3 oz (75g) vegetable margarine
4 teaspoons mixed herbs
½ pint (275ml) milk (sour if possible)

Heat the oil in a heavy based pan and sauté the onions until golden brown - the longer this takes, the better. Add the remaining ingredients and bring to the boil. Reduce the heat, cover and simmer for 20 minutes.

Mix together the flour and margarine until they resemble fine breadcrumbs. Stir in the herbs and add the milk gradually to form a soft dough. Turn out on to a floured surface and gently form into a smooth round about 2 inches (5cm) deep. Score into quarters with a sharp knife and place on a baking sheet. Bake in the oven at 425F/220C/Gas 7 for 30-35 minutes until slightly risen and golden brown. Cool and cut through the scored lines.

SWEET POTATO PATTIES WITH STIR-FRIED VEGETABLES

Serves 4

1½ lbs (700g) sweet potatoes, chopped
1 tablespoon oil
1 large clove garlic, finely chopped
1 onion, finely chopped
2 teaspoons curry powder
4 tablespoons mango chutney
pinch grated nutmeg
salt and pepper to taste
1 egg, beaten
3 oz (75g) flaked almonds
oil for shallow frying
1 orange, segmented

½ inch (1cm) fresh root ginger
mixture of finely chopped vegetables: eg white
and red cabbage, spinach, courgettes, carrots, red
pepper, celery, radishes, broccoli and mushrooms
soy sauce and seasoning to taste

Steam or boil the sweet potatoes for 15-20 minutes until tender. Drain well and mash. Heat the oil in a pan, add the garlic, onion and curry powder and cook until softened. Add to the potato with the chutney, nutmeg, salt and pepper.

Shape the mixture into 4 patties, dip in the beaten egg and cover with flaked almonds. Shallow-fry in hot oil for 5 minutes on each side until golden brown. Garnish with orange segments.

Heat some oil in a large frying pan or wok. Grate the ginger into the oil and cook slightly. Add the vegetables and toss until well heated through (about 4 minutes). Add the soy sauce and coat all the vegetables. Season and serve immediately.

YORKSHIRE CURD TART

Serves 6-8

FOR THE PASTRY:
8 oz (225g) wholemeal flour
4 oz (125g) margarine
3 tablespoons water

FOR THE FILLING:
1 lb (450g) curd cheese
2 oz (50g) softened butter
4 eggs, beaten
2 tablespoons caster sugar
2 tablespoons golden syrup
2 oz (50g) currants
grated zest of 2 lemons

Rub the flour and margarine together until the mixture resembles fine crumbs. Add sufficient water to give a soft but manageable dough. Roll out the dough on a floured surface and line an 8 inch (20.5cm) flan case.

Mix all the filling ingredients together and put in the pastry case. Bake in the oven at 350F/180C/Gas 4 for about 45 minutes until golden brown and firm to the touch. Serve warm or cold.

John Davis

ex-JOLLYS · NEWTON POPPLEFORD

At Jollys we cater for all tastes but interesting vegetarian dishes are a speciality. Fifty per cent of main courses are suitable for vegetarians, as well as the majority of starters and desserts. Many regular customers choose from the vegetarian selection without being vegetarian themselves - they are keen to sample dishes which they may not have the inclination to tackle at home. The simple philosophy is to give guests a comfortable, relaxing evening to remember, with the emphasis on quality and value for money. We feel that we are able to offer an easy introduction to the pleasures of vegetarian dining and staff are always on hand to explain the nature and availability of ingredients used. Some customers will be trying a complete vegetarian meal for the first time and our aim is to show them what can be achieved without using meat.

BAKED STUFFED MUSHROOMS WITH A MINTED CUCUMBER DRESSING

Serves 4

10 medium-large open cap mushrooms
2 teaspoons olive oil
2 sticks celery, roughly chopped
3 cloves garlic, finely chopped
2 teaspoons capers
3 oz (75g) wholemeal breadcrumbs
1 tablespoon fresh parsley, chopped
2 tablespoons lemon juice
1 tablespoon sunflower seeds
pinch cayenne pepper
salt and pepper
6 oz (175g) grated Cheddar cheese

FOR THE DRESSING:
8 oz (225g) plain yogurt
1 tablespoon lemon juice
1/2 cucumber, finely diced
3-4 leaves fresh mint, chopped
1 clove garlic, finely chopped
salt and pepper

Mushroom starters are always very popular and this one is no exception. It can be prepared in advance and simply popped in the oven when required.

Wipe the mushrooms clean and remove their stalks. Select 8 of the mushrooms and lightly steam them for 3-4 minutes to soften them. Set aside on a greased baking tray.

Roughly chop the remaining mushrooms and the stalks. Heat the oil in a pan over a low/medium flame. Add the chopped mushrooms, garlic and celery and cook until lightly browned, stirring occasionally. Tip into a food processor bowl with the capers, breadcrumbs, parsley, lemon juice, sunflower seeds and cayenne. Process until the mixture is well chopped. Add salt and pepper to taste.

Spread the stuffing on the prepared mushrooms, sprinkle with cheese and bake in the centre of a pre-heated oven at 350F/180C/Gas 4 for approx. 15 minutes or until well browned.

Whilst the mushrooms are cooking, mix together all the ingredients for the dressing and season to taste. Serve the dressing with the hot stuffed mushrooms.

SPINACH AND CASHEW LOAF WITH RED PEPPER PUREE

Serves 8-10

6 oz (175g) cashew nuts
3 oz (75g) hazel nuts
3 oz (75g) brazil nuts
6 oz (175g) wholemeal breadcrumbs
1 medium onion, finely chopped
1 medium carrot, grated
1 tablespoon olive oil
2 fl oz (50ml) white wine
1 teaspoon dried mixed herbs
1 teaspoon curry powder
1 tablespoon lemon juice
2 fl oz (50ml) good vegetable stock
1 egg, beaten
1/2 teaspoon grated nutmeg
1 tablespoon soy sauce
salt and pepper

FOR THE SPINACH LAYER:
1/2 medium onion, chopped
1/2 tablespoon olive oil
8 oz (225g) frozen spinach, defrosted and drained
1 oz (25g) butter
3 oz (75g) wholemeal breadcrumbs
salt and pepper
3-4 large white cabbage leaves

FOR THE RED PEPPER PUREE:
1/2 medium onion, chopped
1/2 tablespoon olive oil
2 medium red peppers, deseeded and chopped
1 oz (25g) butter
3 fl oz (75ml) good vegetable stock
salt and pepper

This nut loaf is quite easy to prepare and is guaranteed to impress dinner guests, particularly if served on a bed of the purée.

Chop the nuts in a food processor until fairly fine. Place in a large mixing bowl with the breadcrumbs.

In a frying pan, gently fry the onions and carrot in olive oil until softened. Add to the other ingredients in the bowl. Add the remaining ingredients to the bowl and mix well. Season to taste and set to one side.

For the spinach stuffing, gently fry the onion in the olive oil until softened. Add the spinach and butter, cover and continue cooking over a low heat for 5-10 minutes. Place the spinach mixture in a food processor bowl with the breadcrumbs and process to a thick paste. Season to taste and set aside.

Blanch the cabbage leaves for 1-2 minutes in lightly salted boiling water. Cool in a bowl of cold water and set aside.

Lightly grease a 2 lb (900g) loaf tin, then line

with greaseproof paper or baking parchment (grease again if using greaseproof). Spoon in half of the nut mixture and cover with half the blanched cabbage leaves. Spoon in the spinach mixture and again cover with leaves. Finish with the rest of the nut mixture and press down well. Place the tin in the centre of a pre-heated oven at 350F/180C/Gas 4 and cook for 45 minutes or until firm to the touch.

The loaf can either be served whole by turning out on to a plate whilst still hot or allowed to cool then sliced into portions and reheated when required.

For the red pepper purée, gently fry the onion in olive oil for approx. 5 minutes. Add the red pepper and continue to cook, stirring occasionally, until the pepper is softened. Place the onion and pepper in a liquidiser goblet, add the butter and stock along with salt and pepper to taste and liquidise to a thick purée.

Serve the loaf in slices on a bed of the purée.

OLD FASHIONED BREAD PUDDING

Serves 8

4 oz (125g) soft brown sugar
6 oz (175g) margarine
5 oz (150g) golden syrup
6 oz (175g) wholemeal breadcrumbs
2 eggs, beaten
good pinch nutmeg
2 teaspoons mixed spice
1 teaspoon baking powder
2 oz (50g) self-raising flour
15 fl oz (400ml) milk
12 oz (350g) mixed dried fruit

This is a permanent fixture on our menu and is particularly popular with our more mature customers who remember it from the days of their youth. We serve it warm, sprinkled with icing sugar and accompanied by clotted cream, although pouring cream would be just as good.

Place the first three ingredients in a pan and heat gently, stirring, until melted. Pour into a mixing bowl.

Add the remaining ingredients to the bowl and stir well. Cover and set aside for 1 hour.

Pre-heat the oven to 325F/170C/Gas 3. Grease an 8 x 11 inch (20.5 x 28cm) tin or line with baking parchment and pour the mixture in. Place in the centre of the oven and cook for approx. 50 minutes or until firm to the touch.

Jean Deadman

THE BAYTREE WHOLEFOOD VEGETARIAN RESTAURANT

CLEVELEYS

The Baytree is a small vegetarian restaurant set over a health food shop in the main street of a busy Lancashire seaside town. Decorated in Edwardian style with open fire and soft classical music, we specialise in homemade vegetarian dishes using fresh local produce such as free-range eggs, top quality vegetables and vegetarian cheeses. Dishes include aduki bean or apricot and lentil soups, quiches, currries, pies and casseroles and an extremely naughty selection of puddings such as Squidgy Chocolate Roulade, Pecan Butterscotch Torte or Banana Fudge Pie. Our clientele is about 35% vegetarian, 5% vegan and the majority come simply because they enjoy the food!

CARROT AND ORANGE SOUP

Serves 4

1 oz (25g) butter
1 onion, peeled and chopped
1 lb (450g) carrots, peeled and diced
1 potato, approx 6 oz (175g), peeled and chopped
zest and juice of 1 orange, plus extra orange slices to garnish
1½ pints (900ml) good vegetable stock
salt and pepper to taste
parsley and cream, to garnish

Heat the butter in a large saucepan and fry the onion gently until soft but not brown. Add the carrots and potato and sweat over a low heat for 5 minutes.

Add the orange zest, juice and stock. Bring to the boil then simmer until the carrots and potatoes are soft. Liquidize and season to taste with salt and pepper.

Serve hot, garnished with a thin slice of orange sprinkled with parsley floating on the top, or with a swirl of cream.

CHILLI SIN CARNE

Serves 4

6 oz (175g) dried kidney beans, soaked overnight,
or 15 oz (425g) tin kidney beans
1 medium onion, chopped
1 red pepper, chopped
1 green pepper, chopped
1 yellow pepper, chopped
2 oz (50g) butter
15 oz (425g) tin tomatoes
2 tablespoons tomato puree
1/2 teaspoon chilli powder
1/2 teaspoon dried mixed herbs (or 1 teaspoon
fresh)
1/2 pint (275ml) good vegetable stock
salt and pepper to taste

If using dried beans, drain, cover with fresh water, bring to the boil, boil for 10 minutes, then simmer for 1 hour until tender.

Fry the onion and peppers gently in the butter until tender, then add all the other ingredients including the drained beans. Bring to the boil then simmer gently for 30 minutes to allow the tomatoes to break down well. Season with salt and pepper to taste and serve with wild rice and a green salad.

LEMON DELICIOUS PUDDING

Serves 4

3 x size 3 eggs
3 oz (75g) caster sugar
1 oz (25g) self-raising flour, sieved
zest and juice of 2 lemons
8 fl oz (225ml) milk
1/2 teaspoon salt
1 oz (25g) icing sugar

Separate the eggs into 2 bowls. Add the caster sugar to the yolks and beat with an electric whisk until very pale and leaving trails. Whisk in the flour, grated lemon zest, lemon juice and milk.

With clean, dry beaters on the electric whisk, beat the egg whites with the salt, adding the icing sugar gradually until the mixture is stiff. Stir into the lemon mixture with a metal spoon (the pudding is very sloppy at this stage). Pour into a greased 2 pint (1.1 litre) oven dish and bake at 350F/180C/Gas 4 for 35 minutes or until light golden and set. Serve hot or cold with cream.

Carole Duggan, Joe Quinn

THAT CAFE · MANCHESTER

We regard That Café as a family restaurant and like to try variations on old and traditional recipes as well as experimenting with new ones. The emphasis here is on simple but sophisticated 'real' food served with flair.

LENTIL AND RED WINE SOUP

Serves 4-6

8 oz (225g) red lentils
6 fresh tomatoes, skinned
2 cloves garlic, finely chopped
2 teaspoons tomato purée
dash red wine
water
salt and pepper
parsley

A thicker soup is ideal as a quick main course served with fresh garlic bread.

Rinse the lentils and place in a pan. Fill the pan with water to about $1/2$ inch (1cm) above the lentils and place on a moderate heat. Add the tomatoes, garlic and tomato purée and allow to cook until the tomatoes amd lentils begin to break up. Remove from the heat and blend well.

Return the soup to the pan and add the red wine. Add salt and pepper to taste and garnish with freshly chopped parsley.

MUSHROOM AND CHESTNUT STRUDEL WITH RED PEPPER SAUCE

Serves 4

FOR THE STRUDELS:
2 onions, finely chopped
2 oz (50g) vegetable margarine
1 lb (450g) button mushrooms, chopped
8 oz (225g) prepared and cooked chestnuts, chopped
8 oz (225g) cream cheese
salt and pepper
$1/2$ teaspoon caraway seeds
chopped parsley
2 oz (50g) fine breadcrumbs
1 packet filo pastry
cooking oil

FOR THE SAUCE:
8 red peppers, coarsely chopped
salt and pepper
dash red wine
1 teaspoon tomato purée
sugar (if necessary)

Sauté the onion in the margarine until soft. Add the mushrooms and allow to cook for 10 minutes. Add the chestnuts and cream cheese and cook until all the cheese has melted. Season lightly, then add the caraway seeds, parsley and breadcrumbs. Leave to cool.

Cut the filo pastry into 16 single sheets, approx. 6 inches (15cm) square. Lightly oil each sheet and stick them together, leaving 8 double sheets. Place about 2 tablespoons of the mushroom mixture at one end of one of the double sheets. Fold the sides of the filo over the mixture, then roll along the length, sealing the end with oil. Repeat for each sheet of pastry. Bake the strudels for approx. 25-30 minutes at 450F/230C/Gas 8.

Place the chopped peppers in a pan and cover them with water. Cover, bring to the boil and simmer until the peppers break up. Remove from the heat and blend thoroughly. Pass the sauce through a medium sieve and return to the pan. Season and add the wine, tomato purée, and sugar if the sauce is not sweet enough. Simmer for a further 5 minutes, then serve with the strudels.

BREAD AND MARMALADE PUDDING

Serves 4

8 slices thin bread
marmalade
butter
2 eggs
$1/_2$ pint (275ml) milk
$1/_2$ pint (275ml) double cream
1 oz (25g) sugar
dash vanilla essence
sugar (if necessary)

Remove the crusts from the bread and spread the slices evenly with marmalade and butter. Cut each slice into 4 equal pieces. Grease 4 individual serving dishes and layer each dish with 8 slices of the bread. Blend the eggs in a large mixing bowl and add the milk, cream and vanilla essence. Taste and add sugar if necessary. Fill each dish with the mixture, ensuring that the bread is well covered. Leave in the refrigerator for approx. 1 hour. Bake at 350F/180C/Gas 4 for 1 hour.

Carole Evans

POPPIES · BRIMFIELD

I am a self-taught chef who grew up in a background where garden vegetables were bottled, canned and pickled - I still use as much local produce as I can, including surplus produce offered by my own customers! There are always several vegetarian choices available whether you eat in the elegant surroundings of Poppies restaurant or the comfortable bar.

BAKED AUBERGINE WITH RATATOUILLE

Serves 4

2 aubergines
olive oil
1 red, 1 yellow, 1 green pepper
1 onion
2 courgettes
1 clove garlic, finely chopped
salt and black pepper
10 leaves basil, finely chopped
pesto
Parmesan, grated

Cut the stalks off the aubergines and slice them in half lengthways. Sprinkle the cut sides with salt and leave for $1/2$ hour to extract the bitter juices. Wipe the salt off the aubergines, pour over some olive oil and place in a pre-heated oven 400F/200C/Gas 6 for 15-20 minutes.

Place the peppers in a roasting tin and pour some olive oil over them. Place in a pre-heated oven for about 15 minutes, turning them half way through the time, until the skin begins to scorch. Remove from the oven and allow to cool.

Dice the onion and courgettes and soften in a little olive oil with the garlic. When softened, remove from the heat and allow to cool. Cut the peppers in half, remove the stalk, skin and seeds and cut into even dice. Mix the peppers with the onion and courgette mixture, season well with salt and black pepper and stir in the chopped basil.

Place the aubergines cut side up in a baking dish, spread a little pesto over and spoon on the pepper mixture. Sprinkle with grated Parmesan and bake in a pre-heated oven for about 15 minutes.

SPINACH AND PINE KERNEL PIES

Serves 4

1 lb (450g) soft curd cheese
1 oz (25g) toasted pine kernels, plus extra for sprinkling
2 tablespoons milk
1 teaspoon ground nutmeg
2 egg yolks
4 oz (125g) spinach, finely chopped
4 sheets filo pastry
melted butter

Mix the curd cheese together with the pine kernels, milk, nutmeg and egg yolks. Cook the spinach until tender, squeeze out the excess liquid and add to the cheese mixture.

Butter each sheet of filo pastry, cut a strip from the narrow side of each sheet and reserve for later use. Cut the remainder of each sheet into 6 squares. Lay the squares on top of each other at different angles, to form a star shape. Repeat for each sheet. Place the sheets of pastry, butter side down, in individual 4 inch (10.5cm) loose bottomed tins. Fill the centre with the cheese mixture and place the reserved pieces of filo over the top to cover the mixture. Fold the edges over into the centre and sprinkle a few pine kernels over the top. Place in a pre-heated oven at 400F/200C/Gas 6 for 15-20 minutes until golden.

SAVOURY BREAD AND BUTTER PUDDING

Serves 4

14 slices brown bread
pesto
8 oz (225g) tasty Cheddar, grated
1 oz (25g) pine kernels, half of them toasted
1 pint (570ml) homemade tomato sauce
5 eggs
4 egg yolks
15 fl oz (400ml) whipping cream
salt and freshly ground black pepper
1 tablespoon Parmesan, grated

Spread each slice of bread with pesto and make sandwiches with the grated Cheddar. Cut off the crusts and cut into 4 triangles. Put one layer of sandwiches in a deep rectangular dish 11 x 7 inches (28 x 18cm). Sprinkle with the toasted pine kernels. Layer the remaining sandwiches on top.

Mix the tomato sauce with the eggs, egg yolks and whipping cream. Season and pour over the sandwiches. Sprinkle over the grated Parmesan and remaining pine kernels.

Place in a bain-marie in a pre-heated oven (325F/170C/Gas 3) for about 40 minutes until golden and firm to the touch.

Joan Fikkert

Herbs was opened in 1980 at the Healthy Life Natural Food Centre, with the aim of enabling customers to sample the products available in their Health Food Shop and to demonstrate how natural wholefoods can produce tasty and nourishing dishes. Unadulterated wholefoods are used and as far as possible local produce is chosen. Many customers are vegetarian but many are not; they simply enjoy tasty, nutritious food.

POTATO AND FINE HERB SOUP

Serves 6

3 onions
2 cloves garlic, crushed
2 oz (50g) margarine
2 lbs (900g) old potatoes, peeled and quartered
1/2 teaspoon fresh parsley, finely chopped, plus extra to garnish
1/2 teaspoon fresh chives, finely chopped
1/2 teaspoon fresh sage, finely chopped
2 bay leaves
pinch powdered cloves
2 pints (1.1 litres) vegetable stock
1/2 pint (275ml) milk
2 fl oz (50ml) cream

Lightly sauté the onions and garlic in the margarine but do not allow to brown. Add the potatoes, herbs and stock and cook for approximately 40 minutes or until the potatoes are cooked.

Liquidise the soup until smooth, return to the pan and add the milk and cream. Adjust the seasoning and reheat gently but do not allow the soup to boil. Garnish with chopped parsley.

LEEK AND STILTON PANCAKES

Serves 4

FOR THE BATTER:
1/2 pint (275ml) milk
1 egg
4 oz (125g) wholemeal flour
pinch salt
oil

FOR THE FILLING:
1 onion, chopped
1 lb (450g) leeks, washed well and cut into 1 inch (2.5cm) pieces
1 clove garlic, crushed
1 oz (25g) margarine

2 oz (50g) margarine
2 oz (50g) wholemeal flour
$\frac{1}{2}$ pint (275ml) milk
$\frac{1}{2}$ vegetable stock cube
4 oz (125g) Stilton, grated or crumbled
roasted, flaked almonds, to garnish

To make the pancakes, blend the milk and egg, then slowly add the flour and salt, still blending, until smooth. Leave to stand for 30 minutes.

Meanwhile sauté the vegetables for the filling in the margarine until tender but do not allow to brown.

To make the sauce, melt the margarine, stir in the flour and allow to cook for a minute. Remove from the heat and gradually stir in the milk and stock cube. Return to the heat and slowly bring to the boil, stirring all the time. Add the Stilton, still stirring well. Adjust the seasoning.

Heat the oil in the frying pan and cook the pancakes. Add the sauce to the filling and stir gently until the leeks are coated. Divide this mixture between the pancakes, fold and garnish with roasted flaked almonds.

TOFFEE WALNUT FLAN

Serves 6-8

6 oz (175g) wholemeal shortcrust pastry
4 oz (125g) butter
4 oz (125g) soft brown sugar
3 eggs
4 tablespoons golden syrup
juice of $\frac{1}{2}$ lemon
$\frac{1}{2}$ teaspoon ground cinnamon
5 oz (150g) walnut halves

FOR THE TOFFEE SAUCE:

1 oz (25g) butter
1 oz (25g) soft brown sugar
2 tablespoons golden syrup

whipped double cream for decoration

Line an 8 inch (20.5cm) loose bottomed flan tin with the pastry and chill for 15 minutes.

Beat the butter and sugar until creamy, then add the eggs and mix well. Fold in the syrup, lemon juice and cinnamon. Finely chop 4 oz (125g) of the walnuts, reserving the rest for the topping. Add to the mixture and pour into the prepared pastry case.

Bake for 30-40 minutes in a preheated oven at 350F/180C/Gas 4 until the filling is firm and golden brown.Cool.

Make the toffee sauce by putting the butter, sugar and syrup into a pan. Stir over a low heat until melted, then increase the heat and boil until golden. Remove from the heat and stir in the reserved walnuts - when coated remove them and keep for decoration.

Pour the sauce over the flan and allow to cool before decorating with whipped cream and the toffee-coated walnuts.

Alison Fife

THE STANNARY · MARY TAVY

As can be seen to some extent from these recipes, the aim at The Stannary is to use some of the less familiar ingredients and unusual combinations to create highly individual food; these are integrated on the menu with some dishes that could still be described as 'gourmet' but which people can feel safe with if they are not keen to experiment, perhaps on a first visit. (All the food is vegetarian yet most of our customers aren't). Although superb quality fresh fruits and vegetables are essential, some wild ingredients from the garden and hedgerows are particularly useful and that applies equally to the Stannary Country Wines which my partner, Michael Cook, creates to give added interest to the drinks list. Michael also makes wonderful chocolates. As dining out should always be special, our aim is to provide not just very good food, but also elegant surroundings and a personal touch.

MERMAID'S PURSE

Serves 4

FOR THE PARCELS:

1 packet (10 square sheets) nori
3/4 oz (15g) white (unbleached) flour
3/4 oz (15g) butter or margarine
pinch turmeric
1 teaspoon tomato purée
2 1/2 fl oz (70ml) water
4 oz (125g) baby sweetcorn

FOR THE BISCUITS:

1 oz (30g) vegetarian Cheddar cheese
3 oz (80g) white (unbleached) flour
1 1/2 oz (40g) butter or margarine
1 sheet of the nori

green salad, to serve

This dish resembles the Mermaid's Purse found on the beach, but is actually created from a more edible variety of seaweed, available in delicatessens and ethnic shops in dried sheet form (make sure you get the square-ish ones). The slices of baby sweetcorn are like golden coins in the purse!

Grill each sheet of nori one at a time on a baking tray under a very hot grill, for just a couple of seconds each side, changing it from almost black to a translucent green. Cut each sheet into quarters with scissors.

Make a roux with the flour and butter. Add the turmeric, tomato purée and water and cook through to make a thick golden sauce. Chop the baby sweetcorn into fine 'coins' and mix into the sauce.

To create the parcels you need to work at a reasonable pace, as once damp, the nori will fall apart if left too long; you will find you have more sheets than needed, so some experimentation will be possible.

With a pastry brush, dampen the surface of a chopping board. Place two of the nori quarters, rough side up, on the board and brush with water. Place a good teaspoonful of the mixture on one square and fold one corner two-thirds of the way across the diagonal, followed by the opposite corner to the edge, then do the same with the other corners, creating a square or rectangular parcel (don't worry about any untidiness at this stage). Place this parcel, with the join sides down, diagonally on the other nori sheet and press gently into a good shape before repeating the wrapping stage. Turn over and give a final press into shape (as the nori dries out it will shrink a little and make the parcel tighter and the joins almost invisible). Repeat until you have made three parcels for each person.

For the biscuits, put the cheese, flour and 4 quarter sheets of nori (not dampened) into a mixer with a sharp blade and chop until the cheese seems to have disappeared and the nori is in fine flakes. Add the butter and keep mixing until a dough is formed. Divide into 4 or 8 and press into a mould or shape by hand to resemble shells. Bake at 400F/200C/Gas 6 for about 10 minutes until firm.

Serve the parcels at room temperature and the biscuits preferably slightly warm, on a sea of green salad.

FRAGRANT PALM HEARTS

Serves 4

2 rosehip tea bags
9 oz (250g) basmati rice
1 tin palm hearts (14 oz/400g drained weight)
3½ oz (100g) cream cheese
1 oz (25g) cornflour
7 fl oz (200ml) milk
1 tablespoon rosewater
½ teaspoon tomato purée (optional, for colour)
handful pink rose petals (fresh or dried)
1-2 tablespoons pink peppercorns
puff pastry (optional)

crunchy fresh vegetables, cooked 'al dente', to serve

This is an ideal dish (all pink and scented) for Valentine's Day – but of course the quantities will need to be halved! The main mixture is very soft and benefits from a little rice accompaniment, but is better still with good vegetables as well. Palm hearts are, I believe, only available tinned in this country, but are still a wonderful ingredient. If using fresh rose petals (which is preferable of course) make sure thay haven't been sprayed; if they are not available you can get dried rose petals from home-brew shops but you will have to pick out the bits of leaves and twigs. Pink peppercorns aren't actually pepper but are aromatic dried berries and can be used whole.

Pour boiling water on to the rosehip teabags and use this tea to cook the rice (the amount of water required will depend on your method of cooking rice).

Rinse 14 oz (400g) of the palm hearts and cut into ¼ inch (0.5cm) discs (don't worry that many will break up). Mix together the cream cheese and cornflour, and add the milk, rosewater and tomato purée. Cook in a microwave or over a gentle heat until the sauce has thickened. Add the petals (which will have needed soaking for half an hour if dried rather than fresh) and pink peppercorns, then add the palm hearts. Heat gently just before serving with the rice.

As a finishing touch make hearts from puff pastry, brushed with tandoori paste or beetroot juice to give a pink finish to match the rest of the dish.

CITRUS AND WALNUT WEDGE

Serves 4

1 small orange (thin skinned)
2 fl oz (50ml) orange juice
3 oz (75g) walnuts
4 oz (125g) sugar
4 oz (125g) butter
4 oz (125g) wholemeal flour
3 oz (75g) porridge oats
1/2 teaspoon ground cinnamon
1/2 teaspoon baking powder
2 small free range eggs
3 oz (75g) raw cane sugar
5 fl oz (150ml) lemon juice
fruit to decorate (optional)

natural yoghurt or cinnamon flavoured custard, to serve

This is a sharp yet sweet and sticky sort of very flavoursome cake.

Cut the orange into pieces and remove any pips. Put it with the orange juice into an electric blender and reduce to pulp. Chop the walnuts to breadcrumb-sized pieces.

In a food processor mix everything except the raw cane sugar and lemon juice. Keep mixing for several minutes until the mixture looks lighter in colour and creamy. Spread, with a small dip in the centre, in an appropriate cake tin, preferably square. Bake on a low heat for about 20 minutes.

Mix the raw cane sugar and lemon juice, heating gently to help the sugar dissolve. Allow the cake to cool for a few minutes in its tin then turn it upside down on to a plate. Prick holes all over. While it is still warm, pour the lemon syrup over the cake, allowing it to soak in.

Cut into quarters (corner to corner if square). Decorate with fruit if wanted. Warm gently to serve.

Ann Fitzgerald

The background to vegetarian food at the Farmhouse Kitchen is my lifelong love of Chinese, Indian, Japanese and Indonesian food, as well as a strong Italian influence. The eastern influence elevates the most mundane vegetable to the status of prime meat, offering a challenge to the cook to make something really special. From Italian cooking comes pasta which is such a natural for vegetarian dishes, quite apart from Italian cheeses, rice, wild mushrooms, tomatoes and olive oil.

VEGETABLE RAVIOLI WITH TOMATO AND BASIL SAUCE

Serves 6-8

FOR THE VEGETABLE FILLING:
2 shallots, thinly sliced
1 lb (450g) ripe tomatoes, chopped
4 oz (125g) courgettes
8 oz (225g) skinned aubergine, diced
1 skinned red pepper, diced
olive oil
garlic
salt and pepper

FOR THE PASTA DOUGH:
10 oz (275g) plain flour
3 large eggs
salt

FOR THE TOMATO SAUCE:
2 or 3 shallots, thinly sliced
2 lbs (900g) ripe tomatoes, chopped and deseeded
olive oil

3 glasses red wine (eg Barbera from Piedmont)
softened butter kneaded with flour
salt and pepper
fresh basil
Parmesan cheese, to serve

Sauté the shallot, tomato, courgette, aubergine, red pepper, garlic and seasoning in the olive oil. Sweat the mixture down for 15-20 minutes and set aside to cool.

Blend the pasta ingredients in a food processor until a lump of firm, shiny dough is formed. A little more flour may be necessary to get the smooth, elastic finish - this will depend on the size of the eggs. Wrap the dough in clingfilm and refrigerate for at least $1/_2$ hour.

Cut the dough into 4, dust the work surface and a rolling pin - the long thin ones are best - and roll out the dough , rotating by quarter turns as you work until you achieve the required thickness. Alternatively you can roll out the dough using one of the pasta machines which are now widely available - set the rollers to the widest setting and feed through the floured dough a quarter at a time.

Cut this rolled out quarter of the dough in half and on one half spoon heaps of the vegetable filling about 1 inch (2.5cm) apart. Brush the whole of the other half with cold water and carefully lay this sheet over the other, firmly sealing the paste between each mound, then cut the ravioli into separate sachets. Repeat the whole process with as much of the dough as you need. This is the smallest amount it is practicable to make but any remaining may be frozen. To make the sauce, sauté the shallot and tomatoes in olive oil. Add some red wine and simmer for about 15 minutes until the liquid is reduced to a thin sauce. Thicken to the required consistency by stirring in some kneaded butter; add some coarsely shredded basil leaves, season with salt and pepper and simmer gently while you cook the ravioli.

Bring a large pan of salted water to the boil and drop in the ravioli, keeping the water at a rolling boil. When cooked (3-4 minutes) the ravioli will float to the surface. Lift them out with a slatted spoon and keep warm. When they are all ready, dish the ravioli into the centre of a hot plate, grate some Parmesan cheese over them, spoon the sauce around the edge of the plate and serve with more Parmesan handed separately. As a variation, deep-fry the ravioli instead of boiling them, or do half and half for a really stylish starter.

RED DRAGON PIE

Serves 4-6

8 oz (225g) aduki beans
1 large onion, sliced
2 sticks celery, sliced
2-3 carrots, cut into thin batons
red wine
4 tablespoons soy sauce
black pepper
olive oil
cooked mashed potato

Soak the aduki beans in water for about 6 hours. Simmer them in water for about 30-40 minutes until soft but not mushy. After about 20 minutes start to sauté the onion until soft, then add the celery and carrots.

Strain the aduki beans and reserve the liquor to use as vegetable stock in another dish - it would give too strong a flavour here. Add the beans to the other ingredients in the pan and add enough red wine almost to cover, together with the soy sauce and black pepper (no salt because of the soy sauce).

Simmer with the lid off the pan for about 30 minutes, adding more red wine if the mixture becomes too dry and more soy sauce to taste, if required. Do not allow the mixture to become too dry as it will lose a bit more liquid in the final cooking stage and it must be juicy when you dish it up.

Pour the mixture into an ovenproof dish leaving an inch or so at the top. Cover with mashed potato and bake in a moderate oven for about 20 minutes or until the potato browns. Serve with spinach, broccoli or another green vegetable.

BREAD PUDDING WITH WHISKY SAUCE

Serves 8

1 large loaf day-old bread
3 pints (1.1 litres) milk
12 oz (350g) seedless raisins
5 fl oz (150ml) whisky
5 large eggs
6 oz (175g) sugar
3¹/₂ oz (100g) melted butter, cooled
2 teaspoons vanilla esence
1 teaspoon salt

FOR THE WHISKY SAUCE:
4¹/₂ oz (140g) unsalted butter
4 oz (125g) sugar
2 large eggs
8 fl oz whisky

Cut the bread into 1 inch (2.5cm) cubes, crusts included. Soak the cubes in milk, in a large bowl, for 2 hours at room temperature, stirring occasionally. In a smaller bowl, macerate the raisins in the whisky for the same time.

Break the eggs into a jug or basin and add the sugar, melted butter, vanilla essence and salt. Whisk to combine well, then pour it over the soaked bread, add the raisins and liquor and mix well. Butter a large ovenproof soufflé dish and tip in the mixture. Cover with clingfilm and put in the fridge overnight.

Next day take the mixture out of the fridge and allow to return to room temperature. Preheat the oven to 350F/180C/Gas 4 and bake in the middle of the oven for about 1¹/₂ hours or until the top is puffed and golden brown.

For the sauce, cream together the softened butter and sugar until light and fluffy, then beat in the eggs one at a time and add the whisky. Put the mixture in the top of a double boiler (or in a basin over a saucepan of water with the basin not quite touching the water) and whisk over a moderate heat until the sauce thickens and the sugar has dissolved. Spoon the pudding into warmed dishes and hand the sauce in a warm jug.

Jackie Gear

In the 1970s, I worked as a scientist in water pollution control. My concern over environmental problems, the third world, and animal welfare eventually led to my resigning my post and working instead for a small charity, the Henry Doubleday Research Association - now Europe's largest organic organisation. For several years I gardened, bottled fruit, made jams and chutneys, baked bread each day, kept bees and chickens, and cooked for the vegetarians, vegans, fruitarians and macrobiotic students who worked at the HRDA. When our headquarters moved from Essex to the Midlands in 1985, I wanted to open a restaurant on site to promote organic food. The dream has become a reality and Ryton Gardens Restaurant is now listed in several good food guides. We are 99% vegetarian but occasionally cook with fish or organic free range meat. Eggs and cheeses used are also from free range livestock. The menu is entirely wholefood and predominantly organic.

JULIENNE OF VEGETABLES HOLLANDAISE

Serves 4

2 oz (50g) carrots
2 oz (50g) peppers
2 oz (50g) mushrooms
2 oz (50g) courgettes
3$\frac{1}{2}$ oz (100g) cauliflower florets
3 cloves garlic
2 tablespoons peanut oil

FOR THE SAUCE:
1 teaspoon lemon juice
1 tablespoon water
salt and pepper
2 egg yolks
3$\frac{1}{2}$ oz (100g) butter

Wash the vegetables, dry thoroughly and cut into matchsticks. Season the peanut oil by adding 3 peeled cloves of garlic and leaving for 1 hour.

Remove the garlic and heat the oil in a large pan or wok. Add the vegetable matchsticks and stir-fry for 1-2 minutes. Remove the vegetables and strain off the excess oil well.

To make the sauce, mix together the lemon juice, water and seasoning in a stainless steel bowl set over a pan of hot, but not boiling, water. Beat in the egg yolks when the liquid is hot.

Add 1 oz (25g) butter, beating well until the sauce begins to thicken. Add the remainder of the butter and beat well. Add a small amount of extra lemon juice to taste if necessary. Remove from the heat and pour over the vegetables. Serve immediately with a little chopped fresh parsley.

MUSHROOM AND WALNUT STROGANOFF

Serves 4

2 medium sized onions
³/₄-1 lb (350-450g) mushrooms
2 oz (50g) butter
4-8 oz (125-225g) walnuts
1 tablespoon wholemeal flour
5 fl oz (150ml) white wine
5 fl oz (150ml) soured cream
sea salt
freshly milled black pepper
chopped parsley
brown rice and mixed green salad, to serve

Chop the onions and slice the mushrooms. Melt the butter in a saucepan and sauté the onion until transparent. Add the mushrooms and walnuts and stir over a medium heat for 2-3 minutes. Add the flour and mix thoroughly, then add the wine. Bring to the boil, reduce heat and simmer, uncovered, for 2-3 minutes. Off the heat, stir in the soured cream and adjust seasoning to taste. Heat very gently to serving temperature.

Serve at once on a bed of freshly cooked rice. Sprinkle with chopped parsley and serve with a mixed green salad.

BANANA AND PEACH VACHERIN

Serves 6

3 egg whites
6 oz (175g) light muscovado sugar
3 oz (75g) ground cashew nuts

FOR THE FILLING:
2 fresh peaches, peeled
2 bananas, peeled and tossed in lemon juice
11 fl oz (300ml) double cream, whipped

Line 2 baking trays with greaseproof paper. Mark an 8 inch (20cm) circle on each. Mark one in 6 segments. Whisk the egg whites until stiff, gradually fold in the sugar until thick and glossy, then fold in the cashew nuts.

Select a piping bag with a ¹/₂ inch (1.2cm) plain nozzle. Pipe on to the first tray in an inward spiral pattern and on to the second tray in 6 wedges, leaving a gap for the meringue to expand. Cook for 30-40 minutes at 375F/190C/Gas 5.

Add most of the peeled and sliced peaches and bananas to the whipped cream and place on top of the round meringue. Decorate with meringue wedges and remaining fruit.

Benedict Harding

CHERRIES BISTRO · BRISTOL

An abhorrence for intensive farming methods converted me to vegetarianism in 1981. My two brothers are chefs and when the family opened the Acorn Restaurant and Wholefood Shop in Swindon, the opportunity arose for me to make a living out of my interests. In 1990 I moved to Cherries in Bristol where a variety of influences inspire the cooking - from the rich colours and flavours of Provence to the subtle spices of Oriental cuisine.

ARAME SEAWEED WITH CUCUMBER AND RADISH MATCHSTICKS

Serves 4

3 oz (75g) Arame seaweed
1 fl oz (25ml) lemon juice
2 tablespoons chopped fresh ginger
1 fl oz (25ml) shoyu
1 fl oz (25ml) sesame oil
1/2 cucumber
small bunch radishes
orange and lemon slices and fresh mint, to garnish

Wash the seaweed well in cold fresh water. Put the seaweed in a pan, cover with water, bring to the boil and simmer for 4 minutes. Take off the heat and cool under the cold tap. Sieve and pour a kettle of boiling water over it.

Mix together the lemon juice, ginger, shoyu and oil and mix with the seaweed in a bowl. Form into nests on small side plates. cut the cucumber and radish into matchsticks and sprinkle over the seaweed. Garnish with the lemon and orange slices and fresh mint.

SPICY CARIBBEAN COBBLER

Serves 4

2 tablespoons olive oil
2 onions, finely chopped
2 cloves garlic, crushed
1 teaspoon chopped fresh ginger
2 teaspoons curry powder
1 teaspoon ground cumin
6 cloves
pinch cayenne pepper
4 sweet potatoes (or yams) peeled and cubed
2 red peppers, sliced
4 thick courgettes, thickly sliced
4 green bananas (plantains), peeled and thickly sliced
4 pineapple rings, chopped
1 tablespoon desiccated coconut
14 oz (400g) tin tomatoes, drained
juice of 1 lime
3 tablespoons dark rum
1/2 pint (275ml) vegetable stock
salt and pepper
soy sauce, to taste
8 oz (225g) self-raising flour

2 teaspoons dried mustard powder
salt and pepper
2 oz (50g) vegetable suet
1 egg, beaten
a little milk

Heat the oil in a large pan. Fry the onion until soft, add the garlic, ginger and other spices and cook for 3 minutes. Mix in the sweet potatoes, peppers, courgettes, bananas and pineapple and sweat for 10 minutes, stirring occasionally.

Add the coconut, tomatoes, lime juice, stock, rum, seasoning and soy sauce. Cover and cook for 1 hour or until tender. Transfer to an ovenproof serving dish.

Sift the flour, mustard and seasoning into a bowl. Add the suet and rub in until the mixture resembles breadcrumbs. Add the beaten egg and enough milk to form a soft dough. Roll out and cut into circles about $1/2$ inch (1cm) thick. Brush with milk and arrange overlapping on top of the curry. Bake in the oven at 425F/220C/Gas 7 for about 20 minutes or until golden brown.

CHOCOLATE MOUSSE WITH COINTREAU

Serves 4

3 oz (75g) butter
3 oz (75g) good quality dark chocolate eg Menier
2 teaspoons Cointreau
2 egg whites
7 fl oz (200ml) whipping cream

Melt the butter and chocolate in a bain marie. When it is hot to the touch, add the Cointreau. Using an electric whisk, whip the cream until it forms stiff peaks. Fold the chocolate and butter into the cream and gently stir occasionally until it starts to thicken.

Whisk the egg whites and fold them into the mixture. Pour into dessert glasses and chill.

Janet Henderson

I started by selling organic vegetables grown on the family farm to friends from the boot of my car. From such simple beginnings my lifelong interest in wholefoods led me to open Hendersons in 1963. An informal, cosmopolitan atmosphere prevails, with the restaurant providing a continuous buffet all day of fresh salads, savouries and sweets prepared with high quality produce.

PIQUANT TOMATO SOUP

Serves 4

2 Spanish onions, chopped
2 cloves garlic, crushed
$1/2$ teaspoon chilli powder
1 tablespoon vegetable oil
1 lb (450g) fresh tomatoes
1 medium tin tomatoes
1 tablespoon tomato purée
salt and pepper, to taste
few sprigs fresh basil, torn finely
5 fl oz (150ml) tomato juice or vegetable stock
2 teaspoons brown sugar
parsley, to garnish

Sauté the onions, garlic and chilli powder in oil until tender. Liquidise the fresh and tinned tomatoes with the tomato purée and add to the onion mixture. Season with salt, pepper and basil.

Top up with tomato juice or vegetable stock if extra liquid is required and simmer gently for $1/2$ hour Add the sugar and stir. Serve garnished with fresh chopped parsley.

VEGETABLE HARLEQUIN

Serves 4

1 small cauliflower
2 heads broccoli

FOR SPICY LENTIL SAUCE:
1 Spanish onion, chopped
1 clove garlic, chopped
1 small fresh chilli, chopped
1 pinch cumin
1 pinch coriander
1 tablespoon vegetable oil
8 oz (225g) fresh tomatoes, chopped
1 medium tin tomatoes
2 oz (50g) red lentils, soaked
salt and pepper, to taste
5 fl oz (150ml) tomato juice (optional)

FOR CHEESE SAUCE:
2 oz (50g) margarine
2 oz (50g) plain flour
generous pint (600ml) milk
8 oz (225g) grated cheese
salt and pepper, to taste

2 oz (50g) grated cheese
2 oz (50g) breadcrunmbs

sprigs fresh coriander, to garnish

Cut the vegetables into florets and boil until al dente.

To make the lentil sauce, sauté the onion, garlic, chilli, cumin and coriander in vegetable oil until the onion is transparent. Add all the tomatoes. Drain the lentils and add to the sauce. Cook until the lentils are soft. Season to taste and add tomato juice if extra liquid is required. Place the sauce in an ovenproof dish, lay the vegetable florets on top and set aside.

For the cheese sauce, melt the margarine and add the flour to make a roux. Stir in the milk gradually and bring to the boil to thicken, stirring continuously. Stir in the grated cheese, season with salt and pepper and pour the sauce over the florets.

Mix together the cheese and breadcrumbs and sprinkle over the top. Bake for 30 minutes at 300F/150C/Gas 2. Serve garnished with sprigs of coriander.

SOUR CREAM WITH DRIED FRUITS AND GINGER

Serves 4

1 lb (450g) mixed dried fruits eg apricots, apples, figs, bananas etc, soaked
2 cooking apples, cored and chopped, or any other fruit as required
2 oz (50g) stem ginger, shredded
16 fl oz (450ml) soured cream

This recipe was created originally to make use of fruits that were past their best, but has become a favourite over the years.

Combine the drained fruit in a bowl with the chopped apples or other fruit. Add half the ginger and half the soured cream. Mix well and transfer to a serving dish. Cover with the remaining cream and the remaining shredded ginger.

Simon Hope

FOOD FOR FRIENDS · BRIGHTON

I find continual stimulus for new ideas or combinations of ideas from vegetarianism, the only truly international cuisine. The excitement and challenge of vegetarian cookery attracts me, as does the concept of bringing the cultures of the world together through cookery and creating more understanding between them. I believe that as time goes by, more and more people will become vegetarian and that vegetarianism, with its roots in caring and kindness, will act naturally as an ambassador to help create a happy and united world.

===

ARTICHOKE HEARTS, SUNDRIED TOMATOES AND FRESH ASPARAGUS WITH CROUTONS AND SALAD

Serves 4

FOR THE VINAIGRETTE:
2 oz (50g) raspberries (fresh or tinned in apple juice)
4 cloves garlic
½ pint (275ml) virgin olive oil
3 fl oz (75ml) lemon juice (or white wine vinegar)
2 oz (50g) brown sugar
2 oz (50g) Dijon mustard
salt and pepper

1 lb (450g) fresh asparagus (sprue rather than jumbo - if using jumbo, trim the bottoms)
4 slices white organic bread
1 oz (75g) unsalted butter
selection of salad leaves: Lollo Rosso, Lollo Bianco, curly endive, Webbs, Gem, chicory, Radicchio, Oakleaf, watercress

8 artichoke hearts preserved in virgin olive oil
8 sundried tomato pieces

FOR GARNISH:
2 oz (50g) raspberries
small bunch chives, chopped
rose petals

Make the vinaigrette well in advance to allow the flavours time to mingle. It will not go off and will give you more time to concentrate on other cooking details. Simply combine the raspberries with the oil, lemon juice, garlic, sugar, mustard, salt and pepper. Test for the right balance and adjust accordingly.

Tie the asparagus and stand upright in a pan of boiling salted water (you may have to wedge them in to keep them upright). Poach for 4-6 minutes depending on the thickness of the asparagus. The tips should not be covered by water, so that they are steamed rather than poached.

Cut the bread into any suitable size or shape. Heat the butter in a frying pan and fry the bread on both sides until brown and crisp – allow to drain. Alternatively, the bread may be toasted.

Assemble the salad leaves on four plates and add the artichoke hearts, sundried tomatoes and poached asparagus, still warm if possible. Garnish with raspberries, chives and rose petals and serve the dressing at the table.

COURGETTES AND LEEKS SAINTE FOYENNE

Serves 4

2 oz (50g) butter (olive oil if vegan)
1 teaspoon paprika
1 large white onion, chopped
3 new leeks, carefully washed and sliced into
1/2 inch (1 cm) sections
1 cep, small and fresh or 1/2 dried, finely chopped
3 medium or 6 small courgettes, sliced into 1/4
inch (0.5cm) diagonal slices
1 small red pepper, cut into 1/2 inch (1cm) squares
1 small green pepper, cut into 1/2 inch (1cm)
squares
1 dessertspoon organic white flour
1/2 pint (275ml) crème fraîche (vegans can make a
roux using soya milk)
handful parsley, finely chopped

3 medium new potatoes, par-cooked and cut into
1/2 inch (1cm) slices
1 oz (25g) butter or olive oil
salt and pepper

This is a lovely fresh summer bake using vegetables only - choose the youngest and freshest that you can!

Melt the butter or olive oil in a deep pan or sauteuse, being careful not to burn it. When just hot enough, add the onion and paprika. When it begins to soften, add the leeks and the cep and cook for a further 5 minutes. Add the courgettes and peppers and cook for a further 10 minutes or until they start to soften.

Sprinkle with the flour, making sure it is evenly distributed. Stir in the crème fraîche (or vegan roux) and parsley, then heat through and quickly remove from the heat. Adjust the seasoning and pour the mixture into a metal or pottery baking dish, about 12 ins (30.5cm) x 9 ins (23cm) x 3 ins (7.5cm).

Wash the sauteuse and dry thoroughly before re-using for the sautéed potatoes. Brown them evenly in the butter or oil, sprinkle with a little salt and pepper and use to top the bake. If you have kept the bake warm it may be served immediately - if not, reheat in a moderate oven for 20-30 minutes.

BLUEBERRY AND CHARENTE MELON AU PINEAU

Serves 4

2 large, ripe Charente (or Ogen) melons
8 oz (225g) blueberries
2 wineglasses Pineau des Charentes

After such a rich meal, it's only right to have a fresh, mouthwatering dessert. Again fresh ingredients are essential and of course the Pineau des Charentes which comes from the Cognac region of France and is quite unique in flavour. A good quality Muscat would be an alternative. If you cannot find blueberries, substitute wild strawberries, or raspberries if not used in the first course.

Halve the melons, scoop out the seeds and replace with the blueberries. Add the Pineau just before serving. Serve with a spoonful of Greek yoghurt and a trickle of honey.

Isa Henderson

Prospect Hill is surrounded by beautiful countryside and we have stunning views over the Eden Valley. An atmosphere of complete relaxation prevails and a full vegetarian menu is available. Our dining area has been created from two painstakingly converted farm buildings - the hay barn with honey-orange coloured stone walls and the adjoining gin-case, a half-round milling room.

HOT AVOCADO FILLED WITH CHEESE AND NUTS

Serves 2

1 avocado
3 oz (75g) low-fat cream cheese
1 oz (25g) hard cheese, grated
2 oz (50g) chopped mixed nuts
1 tablespoon low-fat yoghurt
fresh herbs, for garnish

Halve the avocado and remove the stone. Make the filling by mixing the two cheeses with the chopped nuts and yoghurt; use to fill the avocado halves.

Microwave for 2-3 minutes or grill under a low heat for 4-5 minutes. Serve on a salad of mixed leaves, garnished with fresh herbs.

LIGHT AND FLUFFY COURGETTE ROULADE

Serves 6

$1/_2$ pint (275ml) thick white sauce
grated rind and juice of $1/_2$ lemon
2 eggs, separated
2 courgettes, sliced and blanched
8 oz (225g) low-fat cream cheese

Having made the white sauce, allow it to cool, then add half the lemon juice and grated rind, the egg yolks and three-quarters of the courgettes; mix together well.

Whip the egg whites until stiff, then fold into the sauce mixture. Place on a Swiss roll tin that has been lined with greaseproof or bakewell paper and bake at 350F/180C/Gas 4 for about 45 minutes.

To make the filling, mix together the cream cheese with the remainder of the lemon and courgette and spread over the roulade. Roll up when cool and serve in slices.

STRAWBERRY AND BRANDY BRÛLÉ TART

Serves 8

FOR THE PASTRY:

6 oz (175g) wholemeal flour
3 oz (75g) unsalted butter
1 oz (25g) muscovado sugar
¹/₄ teaspoon cinnamon
1 egg yolk

FOR THE FILLING:

2 tablespoons wholefruit strawberry preserve
12 oz (350g) fresh strawberries, coated in
brandy, halved
3 egg yolks
¹/₂ pint (275ml) double cream
few drops vanilla essence
2 tablespoons demerara sugar

Crumb the butter and flour together and mix in the sugar and cinnamon. Make a well in the centre and add the egg yolk and 4 tablespoons of iced water. Mix to a soft, but not sticky, dough. Use the pastry to line a 7 inch (18cm) flan tin and bake blind at 400F/200C/Gas 6 until firm.

Allow the base to cool, then spread with the preserve and arrange the strawberries round the base, keeping a few for decoration. Mix together the egg yolks, cream and vanilla essence and pour over the strawberries. Reduce the oven temperature to 300F/150C/Gas 2 and bake for 1 hour. Sprinkle the demerara sugar on top and grill for 4-5 minutes. Leave to cool and decorate with the remainder of the strawberries.

Gerrard Hocks

CAFE MONDO · SHEFFIELD

I became a vegetarian in 1961 on the advice of my wife, actress Eve Fleur Taylor, taking into account both the benefits of following a healthy eating regime and the ethics of killing innocent animals for food. I have worked as manager in two Blue Ribbon vegetarian restaurants in the UK, namely Cranks in London and Hendersons Salad Table in Edinburgh. I am currently combining the two strands of my career as an actor and a vegetarian chef in compiling my own cookery book, The O.B. Vegetarian, which is loosely based on vegetarian meals within the film and TV industry.

MELON GERRARD

Serves 2

1 Ogen melon
2 oz (50g) fresh raspberries (or frozen if out of season)
2 scoops orange sorbet
brandy liqueur
fresh mint to decorate

Cut the melon in half, remove all the seeds and carefully scoop out the flesh with a melon baller. Mix the melon balls and raspberries together and refill the melon shell. Pour over a generous quantitiy of liqueur brandy. Chill for 2 hours and serve with a scoop of sorbet and sprig of fresh mint.

VEGETABLE CRUMBLE

Serves 6

FOR THE BASE:
2 lbs (900g) assorted root vegetables: parsnips, swede, potatoes, turnip, celeriac
1 large onion
2 fl oz (50ml) olive oil
1lb (450g) chopped tomatoes
15 fl oz (400ml) vegetable stock
1 oz (25g) wholemeal flour
1/2 pint (275ml) soya milk
4 teaspoons chopped parsley

FOR THE TOPPING:
4 oz (125g) soya margarine
6 oz (175g) wholemeal flour
12 oz (350g) mixed chopped nuts
4 oz (125g) mixed sunflower seeds and sesame seeds

If required you can add 4 oz (125g) grated cheese to the topping, otherwise it is a vegan main course.

Chop all the root vegetables and the onion and sauté them in olive oil in a large saucepan. Add the chopped tomatoes and the vegetable stock. Bring to the boil and simmer for 30 minutes. Add the flour, milk and parsley. Stir over a low heat until the mixture thickens, then transfer to a baking/roasting dish or casserole.

Rub together the flour and margarine until it is like fine breadcrumbs, then add the mixed nuts and seeds. Mix well together, spread over the base and cook at 375F/190C/Gas 5 until golden brown.

GERRARD'S STICKY FINGERS

Serves 8

8 oz (225g) chopped pitted dates
8 oz (225g) chopped dried apricots
1 wineglass brandy
8 oz (225g) dark brown sugar
4 oz (125g) margarine
1 egg
1 teaspoon vanilla essence
4 oz (125g) self-raising wholemeal flour
4 oz (125g) 100% wholemeal flour
2 teaspoons baking powder

FOR THE TOPPING:
6 oz (175g) margarine
10 oz (275g) dark brown sugar
¹/₂ pint (275ml) thick double cream

Soak the apricots and dates overnight in ¹/₂ pint (275ml) water with a wineglass of brandy. Cream together the margarine and sugar, then add the egg and vanilla essence and beat well. Add the flour and baking powder and mix well. Finally add the dates and apricots with the liquid they have been soaking in. Mix together. Grease a square baking tin and add the mixture. Bake in the oven for 35-40 minutes at 350-375F/180-190C/Gas 4-5.

Melt the margarine for the topping in a saucepan with the brown sugar. When thoroughly mixed add the double cream and mix well again, off the heat. Serve the cake either hot from the oven with the topping spooned over or cut into slices and microwave on full power for 30 seconds with 2 spoonfuls of the topping.

Baba Hine

This award-winning hotel, situated in an idyllic country setting, is renowned for the quality of its food. An unexpectedly wide choice is offered on the vegetarian menu, making it an ideal venue when vegetarians and meat-eaters wish to dine together.

MILLE FEUILLE OF AVOCADO AND CHESTNUTS

Serves 4

1 lb (450g) puff pastry
1 lb (450g) chestnuts
2 avocados
1 oz (25g) butter
salt and pepper
2 fl oz (50ml) white wine
2 fl oz (50ml) vegetable stock
2 fl oz (50ml) cream

Roll out the puff pastry very thin and cut into 4 inch (10cm) circles, allowing 3 per portion. Bake in a hot oven until crisp and golden.

Prick, roast, skin and quarter the chestnuts. Peel the avocados and cut into large dice. Sauté the avocados and chestnuts in butter with salt and pepper for about 1 minute. Add the white wine, stock and cream and reduce by half.

To serve, place a puff pastry disc on a plate, put a spoonful of the avocado and chestnut mixture on top, then place another disc followed by another spoonful of the mixture and top with a third disc. Pour the remaining sauce around.

BROCHETTE OF MIXED VEGETABLES WITH WILD RICE AND TOMATO COULIS

Serves 4

selection of vegetables: asparagus, mushrooms, baby turnips, carrots, courgettes, baby sweetcorn, salsify, peppers etc.
olive oil
8 oz (225g) wild rice
1 lb (450g) tomatoes
1 sprig basil
1 teaspoon sugar
salt and pepper

Cut the vegetables into even-sized pieces and sauté them briefly in olive oil with salt and pepper: they should still be crunchy and undercooked. Allow to cool.

Cook the wild rice in boiling salted water. Purée the tomatoes in a food processor with the basil, sugar and seasoning. Sieve and warm through.

Thread the vegetables on to brochettes, brush with olive oil and grill. To serve, place a small pile of rice to one side of the plate, a little tomato coulis to the other, and place the grilled brochette across.

HOT PASSION FRUIT SOUFFLE

Serves 4-6

12 passion fruit
8 oz (225g) caster sugar
1/2 cup water
6 egg whites

Unlike custard based soufflés, these sugar based soufflés 'hold' for about 3 or 4 minutes and so are very easy to serve!

Peel the passion fruit, press the flesh through a sieve and throw out the pips. Boil the sugar and water on a high heat until it reaches the 'small crack' stage (use a sugar thermometer). Remove from the heat and add the passion fruit juice immediately. Allow to cool. This mixture may be kept in the fridge for a couple of days.

Whip the egg whites until very stiff and then fold in the passion fruit mixture. Butter individual soufflé moulds and fill with the mixture up to 1/2 inch (1cm) from the top. Cook in the oven at 400F/200C/Gas 6 for about 8 minutes and serve.

Hilary Howard

Stones Restaurant was opened in 1984 by Hilary Howard in a former stable adjacent to the huge stone circle at Avebury. Since then it has just got busier and more complicated as the restaurant's reputation has spread, and the higher level of trade has encouraged more sophisticated and varied cuisine. 'Busier' means busy; well over a thousand customers a day at peak periods, for whom everything - from a variety of breads to the meal presented here - is made in Avebury by the restaurant team. Like any business, Stones has its principles. Its over-riding concern is with the quality of the food and the atmosphere in which (we hope!) it will all be eaten. But behind the scenes, strong attention is paid to other issues, ranging from the quality of work experience for a young team, to the need for sustainable farming (not to mention keeping a bank manager happy). It is the food, though, that does the campaigning!

NEW POTATO SOUP WITH LOVAGE AND SORREL

Serves 6-8

1 oz (25g) vegetable margarine
1½ lbs (700g) new potatoes, washed and sliced
2 large onions, peeled and roughly chopped
4 fat garlic cloves, peeled and roughly chopped
1 teaspoon salt
handful lovage leaves, chopped
8 fl oz (225ml) medium sherry
3 pints (1.75 litres) vegetable stock
handful sorrel leaves, chopped
freshly ground black pepper

Melt the margarine in a heavy pan on a medium heat. Add the potatoes, onions, garlic and salt and sauté until the onions are beginning to go tender, stirring occasionally.

Add the lovage and sherry and continue to cook until the sherry is reduced by half. Add the stock, bring to the boil, then simmer until the potatoes are tender.

Purée and reheat gently. Two minutes before serving, add the chopped sorrel and season with black pepper.

CHIVE PANCAKES WITH SUMMER VEGETABLE FILLING

Serves 6-8

FOR THE PANCAKES:

5 oz (150g) wholewheat flour
1 teaspoon salt
3 medium eggs, beaten
4 tablespoons (75ml) milk
7 fl oz (200ml) water
4 tablespoons finely chopped chives
sunflower oil for cooking

FOR THE FILLING:

1 cauliflower cut into florets
1 head broccoli
12 new carrots, halved lengthways
about 4 oz (125g) mange-tout or yellow wax beans
1/2 pint (275ml) vegetable stock
1/2 pint (275ml) milk
1 onion, peeled and studded with cloves
few bay leaves
3 oz (75g) margarine
3 oz (75g) wholewheat flour
zest of 2 lemons
generous handful chopped fresh marjoram
4 tablespoons capers
1 teaspoon salt, 1 teaspoon black pepper
1 tablespoon coarse-grained mustard
pinch cayenne
4 fl oz (125ml) double cream
lemon juice to taste

This recipe may look complex, but each stage is fairly straightforward. If there is anything we can guarantee not to make enough of at Stones it is pancakes served in this style!

Start by making the pancakes. Combine the flour and salt in a bowl. Beat in the eggs with the milk, then gradually beat in the water until the mixture becomes a creamy, smooth batter. Stir in the chives. Refrigerate for at least half an hour before using.

Heat a lightly oiled 8 inch (20.5cm) pancake pan until the oil is just beginning to smoke. Ladle in about 4 tablespoons of the batter and swirl until the pan is evenly coated. Cook until the underside turns a light golden brown. Turn over and cook the other side for about 20 seconds. Slide the finished product on to an upside down dinner plate. Repeat until all the batter is used up, wiping the pan with kitchen paper soaked in sunflower oil between each performance. You should have about 8 pancakes and are now ready to make the filling.

Lightly steam a selection of summer vegetables such as the list above. Set aside while you make the sauce. Next, heat to simmering point the stock with the milk, onion and bay leaves. This will be added to the roux.

Melt the margarine in a heavy pan on medium heat and gradually stir in the flour. Cook this roux, stirring all the time for one full minute. Still stirring, gradually strain the milk-stock infusion into your pan. Continue cooking until you have a thick creamy sauce. Remove from the heat and add the lemon zest, herbs, capers and seasonings. Finally stir in the cream and adjust the flavour to taste with lemon juice.

Remove half the sauce from the pan and stir this half into the steamed vegetables. Fill the pancakes with this mixture, rolling them up as you go, and arrange the finished rolls seam-side down in a lightly oiled baking dish. Brush the tops with oil or melted butter. Cover the dish with foil and heat for about 30 minutes at 350F/180C/Gas 4.

Meanwhile, gently reheat the remaining sauce, thinning if necessary to pouring consistency with milk or vegetable stock. Serve the pancakes on individual plates with a little sauce poured over and garnished with a sprig of fresh marjoram or marjoram flowers.

MELON AND PEACHES WITH ELDERFLOWER AND GINGER

Serves 6-8

½ pint (275ml) elderflower wine
1 teaspoon ground ginger
1 oz (25g) crystallised stem ginger, finely chopped
1 firm Charentais melon
1 firm Cantaloupe or Ogen melon
6 perfectly ripe, preferably white, peaches
sprigs of fresh mint

First select an attractive deep bowl, pour in the elderflower wine and stir in both types of ginger.

Cut both melons in half horizontally and remove the seeds. Using a melon baller, cut out as many perfect spheres as possible and add to the wine. Halve the peaches, remove the stones and slice into thin moon shapes. Add these to the bowl together with a few sprigs of mint. Refrigerate for at least 3 hours for the flavours to develop. Garnish with additional fresh mint sprigs.

Derek Jeppesen

ex-GREENHOUSE VEGETARIAN RESTAURANT · LONDON WC1

The Greenhouse was opened 8 years ago by sisters Julie and Angela Haslam. An ever-changing menu of vegan and vegetarian dishes is prepared fresh daily for a very diverse clientele including office workers, actors and actresses from RADA (next door) and the Drill Hall situated above the restaurant, students and staff from London University, and doctors and nurses from University College Hospital. A relaxed and informal atmosphere prevails, which is helped by a counter staff made up of actors and actresses, writers, musicians and artists.

FENNEL AND WATERCRESS SOUP

Serves 6

1 medium onion
1 medium bulb fennel
2 tablespoons vegetable oil
1 medium potato
1½ pints (900ml) water or vegetable stock
1 bunch watercress
½ pint (275ml) soya milk or semi-skimmed milk
salt and pepper to taste

Chop the onion and fennel roughly and fry in the oil until soft. Add the chopped potato and cover with stock or water. Bring to the boil and simmer for 10 minutes. Roughly chop the watercress and add to the stock. Simmer for a further 10 minutes or until the potato is tender. Blend until smooth. Return to the saucepan and add the milk. Season to taste. Reheat gently without boiling and garnish with a sprig of fresh watercress.

GINGER AND CORIANDER VEGETABLE CRUMBLE

Serves 6

1 medium onion
12 oz (350g) carrot
2 medium courgettes
1 large leek
1 stick celery
1 green pepper
½ small cauliflower
2 tablespoons vegetable oil
4 oz (125g) fresh root ginger, peeled and grated
14 oz (400g) tin tomatoes
2 tablespoons freshly chopped coriander
juice and zest of 1 orange
salt and pepper to taste
6 oz (175g) wholemeal breadcrumbs
2 oz (50g) soya margarine
1 clove garlic, crushed
1 tomato, sliced
1 tablespoon olive oil

Slice the onion finely, cut the vegetables into bite-sized pieces and break the cauliflower into small florets. Fry the onion and carrot in the vegetable oil until the onion is soft and transparent. Throw in the rest of the vegetables and stir-fry on high heat until tender.

When the vegetables are cooked, stir in the ginger, tinned tomatoes, coriander and orange juice. Bring to the boil and simmer for 10 minutes. Season to taste and pour into a suitable ovenproof dish. Rub the margarine, garlic and orange zest into the breadcrumbs until a rich crumble mix is produced. Sprinkle over the vegetable mixture. Top with sliced tomatoes and dribble over the olive oil. Bake in the centre of the oven at 375F/190C/Gas 5 for 35 minutes or until golden brown and bubbling hot.

MANGO AND STRAWBERRY TRIFLE

Serves 6

12 oz (350g) stale sponge cake
1 large ripe mango
1 lb (450g) fresh strawberries
1 pint (570ml) pineapple and orange juice
2 tablespoons cornflour
1 pint (570ml) milk
3-6 drops vanilla essence
2-3 tablespoons caster sugar
6 fl oz (175ml) whipping cream

Crumble the sponge cake into a large trifle bowl. Cover with the fruit, reserving some to decorate the top. In a saucepan bring the fruit juice to the boil. Add some water to 1 tablespoon of the cornflour to make a thick paste and stir this into the boiling fruit juice to make a thick sauce. Pour over the fruit and sponge and leave to cool. Bring the milk to the boil and repeat the operation with the cornflour to make the custard. Add the vanilla essence and sugar to taste. Pour over the fruit jelly and leave in the fridge until quite cool. Whip the cream and pipe or swirl over the custard. Decorate with the reserved fruit and serve.

Sheila Kidd

THE ARK · ERPINGHAM

The Ark is a former pub, somewhat off the beaten track, which we have run for the past ten years. Vegetables are home-grown and we have just planted a small orchard with many old apple varieties. Our domestic garden is given over to colourful herbs and shrubs and provides a restful setting for outdoor dining, weather permitting! Carnivores as well as vegetarians are catered for at the Ark and we use the crops of peppers, aubergines, tomatoes, courgettes, Queensland Blue pumpkins etc to experiment with vegetarian food. Gluts of home-grown produce, which always seem to happen at the busiest time of the year, mean we often work into the small hours making our own chutneys, soups, sauces and pesto.

LEEK FILO PARCELS WITH WILD MUSHROOM SAUCE

Serves 6

6 or 12 young leeks
salt and black pepper
freshly ground coriander seeds
1 packet filo pastry
4 oz (125g) butter, melted

FOR THE SAUCE:
half oz (10g) dried cepes
1 onion, peeled and chopped
2 oz butter, melted
1 large clove garlic, crushed
10 oz (275g) flat or other mushrooms, chopped
6 oz (175g) crème fraîche
salt and pepper

Prepare the leeks by trimming the ends and outside leaves. Cut the white parts into 12 x 6 inch (15cm) lengths. Cut part way through each section to facilitate cleaning. Wash well, dry and season well with salt, pepper and coriander.

Take the filo (thawed if frozen) and keep covered with plastic wrap and a damp cloth while working. Cut 3 layers about 7 inches (18cm) square for each leek. Brush lightly with melted butter, laying one piece on top of another. Place a leek on one end and roll up. Push the pastry concertina-fashion in from each end and brush again with butter. Place the parcels on a buttered baking sheet and bake at 400F/200C/Gas 6 for 10 minutes. Reduce the heat to 350F/180C/Gas 4 and cook for another 10-15 minutes until the pastry is golden and feels tender.

To make the sauce, soak the dried cepes in hot water for 30 minutes. Strain through muslin and chop the cepes, reserving the flavoured water. Soften the onion in melted butter until tender and add the garlic, chopped cepes and mushrooms. Stir for a minute before adding the reserved mushroom juice. Simmer, covered, for 10-15 minutes. Remove the lid and allow any excess moisture to evaporate. Add the crème fraîche and seasoning to taste and simmer for a further 5 minutes.

Serve two parcels for each person with a little sauce on the side of the plate and more sauce served separately.

RAGOUT OF BLACK BEANS, AUBERGINE, COURGETTE, TOMATO AND HERBS WITH A RED PEPPER MARMALADE

Serves 6

FOR THE MARMALADE:
12 red peppers, halved and seeded
6 large tomatoes, skinned and seeded
2 large onions, peeled and quartered
6 large cloves garlic, peeled
4 fl oz (125ml) red wine vinegar
2-3 teaspoons sugar
salt and pepper
8 oz (225g) black beans, soaked for 6 hours
2 bay leaves
sprig of thyme
salt
2 onions, sliced
3 cloves garlic, chopped
olive oil
1 lb (450g) aubergine
12 oz (350g) courgettes
1 1/4 lbs (550g) large, ripe tomatoes
4 sun-dried tomatoes
1 teaspoon dried oregano
half teaspoon dried thyme
seasoning
Italian parsley and fresh coriander for garnish

To make the marmalade, place the prepared vegetables in a large baking dish and cover with foil. Bake in the oven at 450F/230C/Gas 8 for 50-70 minutes or until completely soft. Puree in a processor then sieve and season with vinegar, sugar, salt and pepper to taste.

Drain the soaked beans. Cover with fresh water, add bay leaves and thyme, bring to the boil and simmer for 45-60 minutes, adding 2 teaspoons salt for the last 10 minutes. Drain and taste for seasoning.

Meanwhile soften the onions and garlic in olive oil in a covered pan until tender. Cut the aubergine and courgettes into 3/4 inch (1.5cm) chunks, add to the pan and stir until partly cooked, adding more olive oil if necessary.

The tomatoes in the meantime should be skinned, seeded and roughly chopped. Cut the sun-dried tomatoes into pieces with scissors. Add the tomatoes and herbs to the pan and continue cooking until tender. Season with salt and pepper and add a little sugar if necessary.

Combine the vegetables with the beans, arrange in a serving dish and stir in some of the marmalade. Garnish with chopped Italian parsley and fresh coriander if liked. Serve more marmalade separately with a crisp salad of mixed leaves, fennel, orange and onion.

BLACKCURRANT SPONGE PUDDING WITH A HONEY CUSTARD

Serves 6

1 lb (450g) fresh or frozen blackcurrants
3-4 oz (75-125g) sugar
juice of 1 orange
4 oz (125g) soft butter
4 oz (125g) caster sugar
2 eggs, beaten
6 oz (175g) self-raising flour
half teaspoon salt
a little milk or gin

FOR THE CUSTARD:
5 egg yolks
1 rounded tablespoon honey
1 pint (570ml) milk and single cream mixed

Put the prepared blackcurrants in a suitable baking dish, well-buttered. Sprinkle the sugar and orange juice over them.

Beat the butter and sugar together until light and fluffy. Add the beaten egg little by little, beating after each addition. Fold in the flour sifted with the salt and a little gin (for a good flavour) or milk to a soft consistency. Spread over the blackcurrants and bake at 350F/180C/Gas 4 for 45-55 minutes or until golden and shrinking from the sides of the dish.

To make the custard, blend the egg yolks and honey in a basin. Bring the milk to the boil and pour on to the yolks, whisking well. Place over a pan of hot water and stir until thickened slightly.

Eluned Lloyd

CNAPAN · NEWPORT

We are fortunate in having loyal guests who return to our restaurant with rooms year by year to enjoy the relaxed family atmosphere and to sample the very varied menu. It is interesting to note a continuing increase in those actually asking for the Vegetarian Menu, which has provided a great incentive to be inventive and take greater liberties with non-meat ingredients. Wholefood lunches at Cnapan have stood the test of time and we put a lot of thought into planning the evening meal with something to please everyone.

SPINACH AND MIXED CHEESES TOPPED WITH HARD-BOILED EGG

Serves 4

FOR THE CHEESE SAUCE:
1½ oz (40g) butter
1½ oz (40g) flour
1 teaspoon coarse grained mustard
1 pint (570ml) milk or half and half cream
4 oz (125g) Llanbridy or other mature cheese
1 oz (25g) Parmesan
pinch nutmeg
salt and pepper

1 packet frozen spinach (or the equivalent of fresh)
1 medium onion, finely chopped
2 cloves garlic
1 oz (25g) butter
zest of 1 orange
1 tablespoon cream cheese
4 hard-boiled eggs

salt and pepper
Pencarreg cheese or Brie for topping
garlic breadcrumbs, made by tossing breadcrumbs in butter mixed with crushed garlic

This makes a good starter or light lunch dish.

To make the cheese sauce, whisk the butter, flour and mustard into the milk until smooth and thickened. Add the cheeses, cook gently for 4 minutes and season with salt, pepper and nutmeg.

Defrost the spinach if frozen and squeeze out the water. If fresh, wash well and cook in a little butter until tender. Sauté the onion and garlic in the butter then process with the spinach, orange zest and cream cheese. Spoon the spinach mixture into individual dishes. Lay the halved eggs on top using 1 egg per person. Pour over a portion of the sauce and top with slivers of soft cheese. Sprinkle with garlic breadcrumbs and place under the grill until hot and bubbling.

TROODOS MOUNTAIN PIE

Serves 4-6

FOR THE HUMMUS:
6 oz (175g) chick peas, soaked overnight
juice and zest of 2 lemons
5 fl oz (150ml) tahini paste (or peanut butter or a
mixture of both)
3 garlic cloves, crushed
4-5 tablespoons olive oil
1 tablespoon chopped parsley
seasoning

FOR THE PASTRY:
8 oz (225g) wholemeal flour
salt and pepper
8 oz (225g) self-raising white flour
8 oz (225g) vegetable margarine

FOR THE FILLING:
enough large plump tomatoes to make a couple of
generous layers
basil, fresh or dried (Greek herbs if available)
8 oz (225g) feta cheese

This recipe is dedicated to our beloved Cyprus!

To make the hummus, simmer the soaked chick peas gently for $1\frac{1}{2}$ hours until soft. Drain and keep the cooking liquid. Process the chick peas with the lemon juice and zest, tahini paste, garlic and oil with approx. 5 fl oz (150ml) cooking liquid. Keep the mixture on the firm side. Season well.

To make the pastry, rub the fat into the flour lightly and bind with slightly more water than you would for all white flour. Leave to stand for 15-30 minutes.

Roll out the pastry and use to line an 8 inch (20.5cm) square pie dish (tin is best). Make a layer of slices of tomato, sprinkled with herbs. Follow with a layer of hummus and a layer of crumbled feta cheese and finish off with another layer of tomatoes and herbs. Roll out the remainder of the pastry to cover the filling and brush with egg wash. Bake for approx. 40-45 minutes at 400F/200C/Gas 6 until golden brown.

STICKY SHORTCAKE PUDDING WITH PRESERVED FRUITS

Serves 4-6

FOR THE FILLING:
6 oz (175g) dried apricots
6 oz (175g) raisins
6 oz (175g) crystallised ginger
orange juice
2 apples, peeled and chopped

FOR THE SHORTCAKE:
4 oz (125g) butter
8 oz (225g) caster sugar
1 egg
4 oz (125g) plain flour
4 oz (125g) self-raising flour
a little soft brown sugar
few ground nuts

FOR THE CUSTARD:
1 tin custard
1/2 teaspoon cinnamon
1 tablespoon brandy or sherry

Soak the dried fruits overnight in a little orange juice. Then process with the apples - this should be of a spreadable consistency.

Cream the butter and sugar, add the egg and beat well. Add the sifted flour, bring together and knead on a lightly floured surface until smooth. Divide into 2, roll out and press each piece into a round between 2 sheets of plastic film, to fit an 8 inch (20.5cm) loose-bottomed tin.

Grease the tin and sprinkle with soft brown sugar and ground nuts. Place one of the rounds into the tin and press down. Spread the fruit mixture over the base, then place the second round on top. Bake in a moderate oven for 40 minutes-1 hour. Allow to cool before turning out upside down.

Serve with a 'cheating' boozy cinnamon custard, made by beating in 1/2 teaspoon cinnamon and 1 tablespoon brandy or sherry with a tin of custard.

Val Macconnell and Sharon Moreton

THE MOON RESTAURANT · KENDAL

When Val Macconnell took over The Moon ten years ago (as a complete novice to the restaurant scene!) there was only one vegetarian choice on the menu: Popular demand, as well as my own vegetarianism, eventually led to a menu which is predominantly, though not exclusively, vegetarian, thus bringing along people who might not otherwise be able to dine together. Interestingly, many people who usually choose meat, often order vegetarian dishes, exploding the myth that vegetarian food isn't exciting or substantial. Our blackboard menu changes regularly and we enjoy the flexibility of introducing new dishes .

FRESH PEACH WITH CURRY MAYONNAISE

Serves 4

1 tablespoon oil
1 small onion, finely chopped
1 level tablespoon curry powder
1 teaspoon tomato purée
2 tablespoons mango chutney, plus extra to fill peaches
juice of ½ lemon
4 tablespoons water
3 tablespoons cream
½ pint (275ml) mayonnaise
4 fresh peaches

lettuce, watercress and parsley, to garnish

The curry mayonnaise is also good with hard-boiled eggs or over a fresh pear half stuffed with cream cheese.

Fry the onion in the oil until soft but not brown. Stir in the curry powder and cook for a further few minutes. Stir in the purée, chutney, lemon juice and water and simmer for 5 minutes.

Liquidise the sauce or strain through a sieve and leave to go cold. Blend together the sauce, cream and mayonnaise.

Cut a fresh peach in half and remove the stone. Fill the cavity with mango chutney. Lay the peach flat side down on a bed of lettuce and spoon over the mayonnaise. Garnish with watercress or parsley.

LENTIL, TOMATO, COURGETTE AND AUBERGINE LASAGNE WITH PARSNIP, YOGHURT AND GARLIC SAUCE

Serves 6-8

olive oil
1 large onion, chopped
6 oz (175g) brown lentils, washed
2 large sticks celery, chopped
1 large aubergine, cubed
15 oz (425g) tin chopped tomatoes
1 dessertspoon tomato purée
½ pint (275ml) red wine
1 dessertspoon basil
1 dessertspoon pesto sauce
2 red peppers, sliced
2 large courgettes, cubed (or equivalent amount broccoli florets)

1 packet no pre-cook lasagne verdi
3 oz (75g) plain flour
3 oz (75g) butter
1 ¼ pints (700ml) milk
6 oz (175g) parsnips (prepared weight)
1 teaspoon nutmeg
6 cloves garlic, crushed
salt and pepper
½ pint (275ml) unsweetened yoghurt or fromage frais
flaked almonds or sunflower seeds, to decorate

Sauté the onions, lentils and celery in the olive oil. Stir in the aubergine until coated with oil. Add the tomatoes, tomato purée, red wine, basil and pesto sauce. When the aubergines are nearly cooked, add the peppers and courgettes. Continue to simmer until the lentils are softening and the aubergines are well cooked. Season.

For the topping, cook the parsnips in ¼ pint (150ml) of milk with the nutmeg, then purée. Make a roux with the butter and flour and stir in the remaining milk gradually to make a thick sauce. Stir in the parsnip purée, garlic and yoghurt. Season. (The sauce is delicious as it is but you could vary it with the addition of some cheese).

In a large ovenproof dish, place a layer of the tomato sauce followed by a a layer of lasagne. Repeat this process, then pour over the parsnip sauce and top with flaked almonds or sunflower seeds. Allow to stand for 10 minutes then cook for 30 minutes at 375F/190C/Gas 5.

RHUBARB, DATE AND ORANGE CRUMBLE TART

Serves 6

FOR THE FILLING:
1 lb (450g) rhubarb, chopped
2 oz (50g) brown sugar
3 oz (75g) dates, chopped
grated rind of 1/2 orange

FOR THE PASTRY:
6 oz (175g) plain flour
4 oz (125g) butter
1 oz (25g) icing sugar
1 egg yolk
3 teaspoons cold water

FOR THE TOPPING:
4 oz (125g) wheatmeal flour
2 oz (50g) butter
2 oz (50g) demerara sugar
1 oz (25g) chopped almonds

Baking apples can be substituted for rhubarb and raisins for the dates.

Cook the rhubarb with the brown sugar and drain off the excess liquid. Stir in the dates and orange rind and leave to cool.

Put all the pastry ingredients into a food processor and run until well blended. Roll the pastry out and line an 8 inch (20.5cm) loose bottom flan case.

Make the topping by rubbing the butter into the flour and sugar until loose and crumbly. Stir in the almonds.

Put the fruit into the pastry case, spoon over the topping and bake for 30-40 minutes at 350F/180C/Gas 4 until golden brown.

Seonaid Martin

HELIOS FOUNTAIN · EDINBURGH

The restaurant is situated at the back of a shop which sells crafts, gifts, toys and books (including many vegetarian ones) and customers can see the food displayed (and indeed the kitchen itself) as they walk through. No ready prepared foods or mixes are used and organic wholemeal bread is bought from a local bakery. Basics such as flour, rice and pasta and many other ingredients are organic. Many vegan dishes and cakes are offered including at least one soup or main dish and most of the salads. Vegetables are always fresh, with the exception of tinned tomatoes, tomato purée and occasionally sweetcorn, much to the appreciation of our customers.

CREAM OF BRUSSEL SPROUT AND ONION SOUP

Serves 16

1½ lbs (700g) onions, chopped
1½ oz (40g) margarine
1½ lbs (700g) potatoes, diced
2 lbs (900g) Brussels sprouts, sliced
2½ pints (1.4 litres) vegetable stock
½ tablespoon thyme
½ teaspoon grated nutmeg
salt and pepper
15 fl oz (400ml) milk
5 fl oz (150ml) single cream

Fry the onions in the margarine until lightly browned. Add the potatoes and Brussels sprouts and cook for a further 5 minutes. Add the stock, herbs and seasoning and cook for about 50 minutes. Purée, then add the milk and cream and heat gently. Check the seasoning.

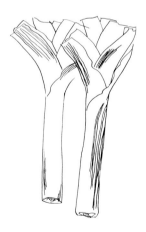

LEEK AND MUSHROOM CROUSTADE

Serves 16

2 lbs (900g) onions, chopped
oil
2½ lbs (1.12kg) leeks, sliced
2½ lbs (1.12kg) mushrooms, quartered
½ dessertspoon marjoram
½ dessertspoon basil
½ dessertspon oregano
1/4 dessertspon thyme
1/4 dessertspoon rosemary
dash shoyu

FOR THE SAUCE:
6 oz (175g) margarine
5 oz (150g) wholemeal flour
2 pints (1.10 litres) soya milk
salt and pepper

FOR THE CROUSTADE:
8 oz (225g) wholemeal breadcrumbs
1 fl oz (25ml) oil
2 oz (50g) sesame seeds
2 oz (50g) sunflower seeds
4 oz (125g) chopped peanuts
salt and pepper

This dish is suitable for vegans.

Cook the onions in a small amount of oil for 15 minutes, then add the leeks and mushroms and cook for another 5 minutes. Add the herbs, shoyu and seasoning and cook until the vegetables are just tender.

To make the sauce, melt the margarine, add the flour, stirring well, and cook for a few minutes. Gradually stir in the soya milk and cook gently until thickened. Season.

Mix together the breadcrumbs, oil, sesame and sunflower seeds, peanuts and salt and pepper. Press down into the base of 2 casserole dishes and bake for 15 minutes.

Mix together the sauce and vegetables, check for seasoning, then pile into the croustade crusts.

CHOCOLATE CHEESECAKE

Serves 12

4 oz (125g) plain chocolate
2 tablespoons honey
2 oz (50g) hazelnuts
8 oz (225g) rolled oats
4 oz (125g) wholemeal flour
6 oz (175g) margarine
5 eggs
1½ pints (900ml) cream cheese
7 fl oz (200ml) yoghurt
2½ fl oz (65ml) single cream

Melt together the chocolate and honey.
To make the base, process the hazelnuts, oats, flour and margarine. Press into the base of a large flan dish.

Process the remaining ingredients together with the chocolate mixture and pour into the flan. Bake at 350F/180C/Gas 5 for 45 minutes.

Carol Ann Marno

COUNTRY LIFE LONDON · LONDON W1R 7LE

Country Life London is unique in several ways. Firstly, exclusively vegan food is served with the exception of a small amount of honey. Secondly, great importance is placed on health education : cookery courses are available in the evenings, based on sound nutritional information provided by our doctor, as well as Lifestyle Management Courses, Stress Control Seminars and a Stop Smoking Clinic.

DUTCH POTATO SOUP

Serves 6

2 garlic cloves, minced
1 cup chopped onions
3 tablespoons oil
2 teaspoons salt
4 cups thinly sliced raw potatoes
4 cups water
$^3/_4$ cup cashew pieces
1 cup tofu cottage cheese
fresh parsley, to garnish

Sauté the first 4 ingredients in a small pan until the onions are clear (the salt draws the juice from the onions). In a saucepan, bring the potatoes and 3 cups of water to the boil. Reduce the heat and simmer until tender (about 20 minutes). Blend the remaining cup of water with the cashews on the highest setting for 1-2 minutes until creamy. Add to the potatoes and boil for several minutes, stirring constantly. Remove from the heat and fold in the sautéed onions and tofu cottage cheese. Serve garnished with fresh parsley.

SUNFLOWER OATBURGERS WITH COUNTRY STYLE GRAVY

Makes 30-35 burgers

3 cups chopped onions
$^1/_4$ cup olive oil
9 cups water
1 cup unfermented soy sauce
1 tablespoon garlic powder
3 tablespoons onion powder
1 tablespoon basil
2 teaspoons oregano
$1^1/_2$ tablespoons ground dill seed
$^3/_4$ cup yeast flakes
1 cup sunflower seeds or chopped walnuts
$1^1/_2$ cups cracked wheat
7 cups regular rolled oats

FOR THE GRAVY:
2 cups water
$^1/_2$ cup cashew pieces or whole wheat flour
1 tablespoon onion powder
$^1/_4$ teaspoon garlic powder
$^1/_4$ teaspoon salt

2 tablespoons oil (omit if using nuts)
3 tablespoons soy sauce or Gomasio
1 tablespoon yeast flakes
1 tablespoon cornstarch

4-6 tablespoons carob powder
$1/_2$ teaspoon salt
1 teaspoon vanilla essence
$1/_4$ cup dessiccated coconut (optional)

Sauté the onions in olive oil in a large pan until soft. Add the remaining ingredients except the oats. Stir together and boil for 5 minutes. Add the oats and mix briefly. Reduce the heat and simmer for 5 more minutes. Cover, set aside and allow to stand for 1 hour.

Divide the mixture into burgers, dipping your hands in water to prevent sticking. Place on a baking sheet and bake at 350F/180C/Gas 4 for 35 minutes, then turn over and bake for an additional 15 minutes.

Blend all the ingredients for the gravy at high speed for 2-3 minutes until creamy. Pour into a saucepan and cook over a medium-high heat until thick, stirring constantly. Serve with the burgers.

Alternatively, the burgers are delicious served on whole grain bread or bun with a lettuce, tomato and onion salad, ketchup or mustard. These burgers freeze well.

CAROB CREAM PIE

FOR THE PIE CRUST:
$1/_3$ cup oil
$1/_2$ cup warm water
1 tablespoon liquid lecithin
1 cup whole wheat flour
1 cup oat flour
1 teaspoon salt
FOR THE PIE FILLING:
4 cups cashew milk
$1/_2$ cup honey or $1 1/_4$ cups date butter
6 tablespoons cornstarch or $1/_4$ cup cornstarch
and $1/_4$ cup whole wheat flour
1 teaspoon coffee substitute

Place the first 3 ingredients in a bowl and beat well with a fork. In another bowl stir together the flours and salt. Add the liquid ingredients to the dry, stirring just enough until a dough is formed. Do not overmix or the crust will be tough. Press the dough together with the hands to form a ball.

To roll out the pie crust, moisten an area of work surface about 12 inches (30.5cm) x 14 inches (35.5cm). Cover the wet area with clingfilm and put half the dough in the centre. Cover with another piece of clingfilm and roll out a 10-11 inch (25-28cm) circle.

Remove the top sheet of clingfilm and place an inverted pie dish in the centre of the dough. Keep one hand on the pie dish while using the other underneath the bottom sheet of clingfilm to lift the dough into the dish. Turn the dish over and press the dough down firmly into the base and sides of the dish. This quantity will make 2 pie shells. Prick the bottom of the pastry shell before baking at 350F/180C/Gas 4 for 20-25 minutes until firm to the touch.

Blend all the ingredients for the filling on high speed until creamy. Empty into a saucepan and cook over a medium-high heat, stirring constantly until thick. Pour into the baked pie shell. Sprinkle with coconut if desired. Cover with clingfilm to prevent a skin forming and chill before topping with soy whipped cream and toasted coconut or coconut dusted in carob powder.

Note: 1 US meauring cup is about the size of an 8oz (225g) cottage cheese carton.

Chris Millward

I regard cooking without meat as a real adventure, leading the cook to think anew and realise just how many things there are to use and the unending combinations available to try out. Instead of cooking to recipes, the menu at Millwards is based on whatever is in season in the market and is kept small to ensure everything is fresh and constantly changing. Free-range eggs and fresh herbs are used and while we are constantly on the lookout for the unusual, the emphasis is on the simple and wholesome.

AUBERGINE ORIENTAL WITH COUSCOUS

Serves 10-12

5 fl oz (150ml) rapeseed oil
2 large or 3 medium onions, chopped
6 large aubergines, washed and chopped into cubes
12 medium tomatoes, skinned and chopped
1 tablespoon freshly ground cumin
1/2 teaspoon pepper
1/2 bunch fresh coriander, chopped
6 cups couscous
9 cups water
good pinch salt

This simple recipe is suitable for vegans; the sauce can be made the day before and indeed tastes even better the next day.

Cook the onions in the warmed oil for a few minutes, then add the aubergines and cook for a few more minutes. Add the tomatoes and cook for 30 minutes on a low heat. Add the ground cumin and pepper to the pot and cook for a further 5 minutes. Remove from the heat, add salt to taste and the fresh coriander.

Place the couscous in a bowl, sprinkle with salt and cover with boiling water. Cover with a lid and leave for 10 minutes, after which it will be ready to serve.

COURGETTE FRITTERS WITH CHILLI SAUCE

Serves 10-12

FOR THE CHILLI SAUCE:
1 Spanish onion, chopped
8 oz (225g) fresh tomatoes, chopped
olive oil
salt and pepper
chilli powder or fresh chillis to taste
FOR THE FRITTERS:
1 lb (450g) courgettes
salt and pepper
1-2 eggs
flour
oil
chopped parsley and slices of lemon, to serve

To make the chilli sauce, cook the onion and tomatoes in a little olive oil with salt and pepper. Cook slowly until really well cooked and add chilli to taste, depending on how hot you like it. Purée the sauce.

Grate the courgettes, sprinkle with salt and leave until they sweat. Wash in a sieve and squeeze out all the water. Place in a bowl, add 1 or 2 beaten eggs, depending on size, add a sprinkle of flour and pepper and mix well together. Wipe a hot pan with oil and fry large spoonfuls of the mixture until golden. Turn over and fry the other side.

Place the fritters on a serving plate with parsley and a slice of lemon accompanied by the chilli sauce which may be served hot or cold.

APRICOT TURNOVERS OR STRUDELS WITH APRICOT SAUCE

Serves 10–12

1 lb (450g) dried apricots, soaked overnight
2 cinnamon sticks
8 oz (225g) ground almonds
dash white wine
FOR THE PASTRY:
8 oz (225g) wholemeal flour
8 oz (225g) unbleached white flour
8 oz (225g) vegetable cooking fat
2 oz (50g) light muscovado sugar
pinch salt
a little water
or 1 packet filo pastry

Drain the apricots, cover with just enough fresh water to cover, and simmer until tender with the cinnamon sticks. Remove the cinnamon and purée the apricots. Using about a quarter of the purée, make a sauce by thinning down with a little white wine. Set aside. Add enough ground almonds to the remaining purée to make a firm paste for the filling.

Make the pastry in the usual way, roll it out and cut into squares or, if making strudels, use $1\frac{1}{2}$ pieces of filo pastry per strudel, brushed with butter if not for vegans. Add 2 good tablespoons of filling for each turnover or strudel. Fold over and seal the edges to make turnovers, or roll up for strudels. Brush with beaten egg (use oil for vegans) and bake in a medium oven for 15-20 minutes until golden.

For the strudel, shake over brown icing sugar (made by grinding demerara sugar in the processor).

Serve just warm with the sauce only for vegans or with the addition of cream or warm custard for others.

Patrick Monney

For the past ten years we have been in the business of providing a relaxing evening in a comfortable and interestingly decorated setting for vegetarian eating out. Our emphasis is on presentation and quality of service and customers can choose from two or three starters and three main dishes with a wide range of salads and desserts.

AVOCADO AND BRIE IN FILO PASTRY

Serves 4

2 avocados
salt and pepper
8 oz (225g) Brie
1 packet filo pastry

TO SERVE:
2 cooking apples
lemon juice
nutmeg
brown sugar
1 tin mango purée or equivalent amount
liquidised fresh mango pulp
1 carton natural yogurt

A colourful start to the meal, this is a simple but delicious starter which excites the palate with the sharpness of the apple contrasting with the smoothness of the purée and the Brie. It also works well cold as a buffet dish or as an interesting supper.

Purée the avocado and season with salt and pepper. Cut the rind off the Brie and dice into pieces (size according to how large or small you require the 'packages').

Take 4-5 sheets of filo pastry, brush each one with oil and stack one on top of the other. Cut into either square or round shapes of the required size, remembering that you need extra for the pinched top.

Place a piece of Brie in the centre of each piece of pastry and add a good spoonful of avocado purée. Lift the edges of the pastry and enclose the mixture, leaving an inch or so of pastry to pinch closed so as to give a parcel effect. Cook in a medium oven until the pastry is crisp and slightly brown.

Slice the apples into wedges and squeeze lemon juice over. Sprinkle with freshly grated nutmeg and then with brown sugar. Place under the grill until the sugar has just melted and the apple is slightly browned.

Peel and liquidise the fresh mango or used tinned mango purée available from Indian shops or delicatessens. Mix 1 part mango with 3 parts natural yogurt - this proportion helps retain the bright colour.

Coat the serving plates with the mango mixture and arrange the apples around the edge. Place the parcels in the centre and serve hot or cold with melba toast.

BUTTERBEAN SATAY

Serves 4

12 oz (350g) butterbeans
1 large Spanish onion, chopped
3 tablespoons oil
1 tin tomatoes
2 red peppers, chopped
2 tablespoons tomato purée
1/2 teaspoon grated nutmeg
1 tablespoon vegetable stock (Vecon)
2 large tablespoons peanut butter
2-3 small hot Jamaican red peppers in jar
5 oz (150g) 5 grain mix or split lentils

This is a lovely combination of flavour and texture, based on an Indonesian recipe, which can be easily adjusted to suit all tastes but is best served on the spicy side and when just cooked. Serve with a green salad and side dish of yoghurt and cucumber or French beans and broccoli with a sprinkling of toasted sesame seeds.

Boil the butterbeans until just soft - there is no need to soak, as is often suggested, as this just splits the beans and removes the skins. Meanwhile fry the onion in the oil until translucent and add the tomatoes, tomato purée, red peppers and nutmeg.

Bring to the boil then add the Vecon, peanut butter and Jamaican red peppers to taste (remembering that they become stronger with cooking). Bring back to the boil, add the 5 grain mix or split lentils to thicken the mixture, reduce heat and simmer, covered, for approx. 20 minutes.

Drain the beans, add them gently to the mixture, to avoid breaking them up, and simmer for another 5 minutes until the sauce is thick.

WHISKY AND GINGER CAKE

Makes 4 cakes

2 lbs (900g) soft brown sugar
3 tablespoons black treacle
12 oz (350g) butter or margarine
2 lbs (900g) wholemeal flour
6 tablespoons ground ginger
3 tablespoons baking powder
1 tablespoon bicarbonate of soda
1 tablespoon salt
7 fl oz (200ml) milk
4 eggs
juice and zest of 1 orange and 1 lemon
3 tablespoons whisky essence or whisky
extra whisky for serving

This freezes well so quantities given are for 4 x 7-8 inch (18-20.5cm) round cake tins.

Gently heat the sugar, treacle and butter or margarine in a saucepan. Meanwhile mix together the flour, ginger, baking powder, bicarbonate of soda and salt in a large mixing bowl. Add the heated ingredients to the bowl and mix well. Add the milk, eggs, orange and lemon zest and juice and whisky essence in that order and mix well - lift to aerate. Line the tins with greaseproof or parchment paper and grease well – otherwise the cakes will be difficult to remove from the tins. Divide the mixture between the 4 tins, spreading it to the edges. bake at 325F/170C/Gas 3 for about 30 minutes.

Leave in the tins to cool then turn out and carefully remove the greaseproof paper. Prick the tops carefully with a fork and pour a tot of whisky over each cake. If freezing, wrap in clingfilm when cold. Serve with a splash of whisky to enhance the flavour and moisture, with whipped double cream with a drop of vanilla added.

John and Pat Millward

M I L L W A R D ' S · B R I S T O L

We were working as jewellers in mid-Wales when we decided to open our own vegetarian restaurant in Bristol in 1987. We wanted to break away from the usual image of vegetarian restaurants: pine tables, animal rights posters etc. and created instead a restaurant with comfortable surroundings, white tablecloths and so on. The cooking is in the modern vegetarian style, keeping the food as light as possible while retaining all the proteins and nutrients. Bristol is a good location because there are excellent organic suppliers in the district who deliver direct, all contributing to our winning the Vegetarian Restaurant of the Year UK 1990-91. Our aim has always been to give value for money using the best ingredients available. Our wine list has about 60 interesting wines, many of them organic.

TWO DIPS WITH CRUDITES

Serves 10-12

FOR THE CARROT AND SWEET POTATO DIP:
1 lb (450g) carrots, peeled
1 lb (450g) sweet potatoes, peeled
3 cloves garlic, crushed
2 teaspoons roasted ground cumin seeds
1 teaspoon cinnamon
4 tablespoons olive oil
3 tablespoons white wine vinegar
pinch cayenne pepper
salt

FOR THE AUBERGINE AND TAMARIND DIP:
1 ¹/₂ lbs (700g) aubergines
2 cloves garlic
1 teaspoon roasted ground cumin seeds
¹/₂ teaspoon ground fennel seeds
pinch cayenne pepper
1 teaspoon freshly grated ginger
2 oz (50g) tamarind, soaked in hot water for 30 minutes and stones removed
8 oz (225g) firm ,plain tofu

FOR THE CRUDITES:
slices of carrot, celery, green, yellow and red peppers, mange-tout, baby sweetcorn, mushrooms, cucumber, cauliflower florets, radishes etc.

Tamarind is available from Indian or good wholefood shops.

For the first dip, boil the carrots and sweet potatoes in salted water until soft. Drain then purée with the other ingredients.

Roast the aubergines and remove the skins or score, wrap in kitchen paper and place in the microwave for 10 minutes. Place the aubergine flesh with all the other ingredients in a processor or liquidiser and blend until smooth.

Serve the dips with a selection of peeled and sliced fresh vegetables.

CHOUX BUNS WITH BLUE CHEESE AND APPLE FILLING ON A CIDER SAUCE

Serves 6

FOR THE CHOUX BUNS:
5 fl oz (150ml) water
5 fl oz (150ml) milk
4 oz (125g) butter
6 oz (175g) self-raising flour
pinch cayenne
freshly ground black pepper
pinch salt
4 large free-range eggs, well beaten
2-3 oz (50-75g) strong, hard cheese
e.g. Cheddar or Parmesan, grated
2 spring onions, finely chopped
4 tablespoons fresh coriander, finely chopped

FOR THE CIDER SAUCE:
1 onion, chopped
oil for frying
1 pint (570ml) cider

FOR THE FILLING:
2 onions, peeled and finely chopped
2 cloves garlic, crushed
2 sticks celery, chopped
oil for frying
2 large Bramley apples
lemon juice
6 oz (175g) blue cheese, grated
black pepper

Heat the water, milk and butter in a microwave or on top of the cooker until boiling. Meanwhile sift the flour with the cayenne, pepper and salt. When the liquid is boiling, add the flour and beat well with an electric whisk. Gradually add the eggs until the mixture is well blended and has a glossy finish, then add the cheese, spring onions and coriander and mix well. Place the dough in a piping bag and pipe on to a greased and watered tray into golf ball-sized shapes - this quantitiy should make 12 buns. Bake in a hot oven (425F/220C/Gas 7) for about 15-20 minutes until well risen and golden.

For the cider sauce, fry the chopped onion in oil until soft, add the cider and cook for 10 minutes. Cool, then liquidise and season to taste.

To make the filling, fry the onion, garlic and celery in the oil until soft (12-15 minutes). Finely chop one apple, grate the other and cover with lemon juice. When the onion is soft, add the cheese, apple and pepper and stir for one minute until the cheese melts. Make a slit in the choux buns, fill with the cheese mixture and bake in the oven at 375-400F/180-190C/Gas 5-6 for about 10 minutes. Serve immediately with the cider sauce.

PISTACHIO NUT PARFAIT

Serves 10-12

3 oz (75g) pistachio nuts
8 fl oz (225ml) milk
1/2 stick cinnamon
1 whole egg plus 8 egg yolks
8 oz (225g) caster sugar
1 pint (570ml) double cream, whipped

Make this dish at least 24 hours before you wish to serve it.

Toast the pistachio nuts under the grill or in the oven for a few minutes. Allow to cool, then chop the nuts by hand or in a coffee grinder.

Simmer the milk with the cinnamon stick for 5 minutes, then cool. Place the whole egg, egg yolks and sugar in a bowl over hot water and whisk until thick (about 5 minutes). Remove the bowl from the heat and continue to whisk until cool.

Strain the milk, discard the cinnamon stick and add the pistachio nuts. When the egg mixture is cool, fold in the nuts and milk and whipped cream. Pour into a 2 pint (1.1 litre) terrine or loaf tin and freeze. Leave overnight to set.

The next day, remove from the freezer and turn upside down on to a serving plate. To unmould the parfait, wipe the tin with a very hot cloth until the parfait drops out. Return the parfait on the plate to the freezer until 5-10 minutes before serving. Slice and decorate as you wish and serve with fresh fruit or any fruit puree.

Boo Orman

After ten years of running Kites, I now cook in the restaurant once a week and have the ultimate responsibility for the menu which changes completely in the spring and autumn. Our recipes have been collected, adapted or devised over the years with the help of the many talented and inventive chefs who have worked at Kites. The terrific increase in the availability of unusual and exotic ingredients, the popularity of overseas travel and an awakening of a desire to experiment in both customer and young chef, has given restaurants a tremendous freedom in menu planning. The danger is to try too hard to be different, and the successful creation of a totally new dish is a very rare occurrence; many of Kites' inventive menu ideas are in fact traditional in their country of origin or were classics in British cookery, albeit several hundred years ago.

EGGS AU MIROIR

Serves 6

1 oz (25g) butter
10-12 spring onions, trimmed and finely chopped
3 handfuls finely chopped parsley
6 large eggs
½ pint (275ml) double cream
juice of 3 small oranges
juice of 2 small lemons
salt and freshly ground white pepper

This recipe is adapted from William Verrall's 'Complete System of Cookery' (1759).

Butter the bottom of a flan dish large enough to hold the eggs.

Sprinkle over the onions and parsley. Carefully break in the eggs, side by side. Mix the cream and the citrus juices, season generously and pour over the eggs.

Bake at 325F/170C/Gas 3 for 15 minutes or until the whites of the eggs are just set.

Serve warm or cold with brown bread or toasted brioche.

SMOKED WENSLEYDALE AND SPINACH PARCELS WITH TOMATO AND CORIANDER SAUCE

Serves 4-6

FOR THE PARCELS:

5¹/₂ oz (165g) walnuts (fresh as possible)
2-3 leeks (white parts only), thinly sliced
2-3 oz (50-75g) butter
2 cloves garlic, finely chopped
salt and pepper
1 teaspoon fresh thyme leaves, finely chopped
¹/₂ teaspoon fresh rosemary, finely chopped
2 teaspoons marjoram, finely chopped
2¹/₂ fl oz (65ml) white wine
large bunch spinach, washed and finely shredded
8 oz (225g) smoked Wensleydale, grated
3¹/₂ oz (100g) cottage cheese
2 eggs, beaten
¹/₂ pack frozen filo pastry
8 oz (225g) melted butter

FOR THE SAUCE:

2 shallots, finely chopped
2 cloves garlic, finely chopped
2 oz (50g) butter
4 tomatoes, roughly chopped
1 tablespoon tomato purée
2¹/₂ fl oz (65ml) sherry vinegar
5 fl oz (150ml) white wine
¹/₂ pint (275ml) water
2 tablespoons superior or light soy sauce
10 fresh coriander leaves, roughly chopped

Preheat the oven to 350F/180C/Gas 4. Roast the walnuts for 5-8 minutes until lightly browned - chop them finely. Soften the leeks in the butter for 2-3 minutes, then add the garlic, salt and pepper, and herbs. Stir in the wine, cover and cook until the leeks are soft. Add the spinach, toss with the leeks and cook until the spinach is wilted. Put the vegetable mixture in a bowl and combine with the Wensleydale, cottage cheese and eggs - test for seasoning.

Brush a sheet of filo pastry with melted butter and scatter with walnuts before placing another layer on top. Continue until you have 4 layers. Cut into squares. The size may vary depending on the size of the filo pastry – normally 8¹/₂-10¹/₂ inches (21.5-26cm). Place a spoonful of the vegetable mixture on each square and roll up to make individual parcels. Bake in the preheated oven for 30-40 minutes.

To make the sauce, cook the shallots and garlic in the butter until soft but not coloured. Add the tomatoes and tomato purée and cook for a further 5 minutes. Add the sherry vinegar and white wine and cook until reduced by half. Pour in the water, cover with a lid and cook gently for 20 minutes. Pass the sauce through a fine sieve and finish by adding soy sauce and the coriander leaves.

Serve the parcels warm, brushed with melted butter, accompanied by the sauce.

ICED SAFFRON, APRICOT AND NUT PUDDING

Serves 8

¹/₃ sachet saffron
1¹/₂ oz (40g) butter, softened
3 slices bread, about ¹/₂ inch (1cm) thick
¹/₄ teaspoon ground ginger
¹/₄ teaspoon ground cinnamon
¹/₄ teaspoon ground cumin
¹/₄ teaspoon grated nutmeg
3 tablespoons muscovado sugar
¹/₂ pint (275ml) double cream
1 lb (450g) fromage frais
2 tablespoons caster sugar
1¹/₂ oz (40g) dried banana flakes
1¹/₂ oz (40g) loose fruit and nut mix
3 oz (75g) no-soak apricots, chopped
2 oz (50g) walnuts, chopped

FOR THE SYRUP:
3 oz (75g) granulated sugar
juice of 3 limes
3 tablespoons clear honey
10 crushed green cardamoms

Steep the saffron in 2 tablespoons of warm water.

Butter the bread generously. Mix the spices together and sprinkle with the muscovado sugar over each slice. Grill until the spiced side is crisp, then leave to cool.

Meanwhile whip the cream until it holds its shape, beat in the saffron and its liquid, the fromage frais and the caster sugar. Fold in the banana flakes, fruit and nut mix, apricots and walnuts. Dice the spiced bread and fold into the cream mixture. Spoon into a 2 pint (1.1 litre) pudding basin lined with baking parchment. Cover with a double layer of clingfilm or foil and freeze.

This may be made well in advance and kept in the freezer but remember to take it out 1-2 hours ahead of serving to allow to soften in the fridge.

To make the syrup, dissolve the sugar in 7 fl oz (200ml) water and the lime juice. Simmer with the honey and cardamoms for 5 minutes, then leave to cool. Skim and strain if desired.

Serve the pudding in wedges (or make in individual containers) with the cardamom syrup.

Juli and Christine Phillips

PIPS WHOLEFOOD BISTRO · GRANTHAM

Identical twins, Juli and Christine Philips, realised a childhood dream when they opened Pips: This is a small, homely restaurant where we aim to provide our customers with an uncomplicated vegetarian menu with recognisable dishes made to simple recipes. Many of our customers are staunch meat-eaters who come along to try something new and often end up as converts!

MUSHROOM SOUP

Serves 6-10

1 quantity vegetable stock (see below)
3 lbs (1.4kg) mushrooms
1 large onion
4 oz (125g) sunflower margarine
5 heaped tablespoons flour
2 pints (1.1 litres) skimmed milk
salt and freshly ground black pepper

chopped parsley, button mushrooms, single cream, wholemeal bread, to serve

Make the vegetable stock by simmering scrubbed celery, carrots and other root vegetables along with chopped onion in 2 pints (1.1 litres) water for 1 hour.

Roughly chop the mushrooms and onion and fry gently in the margarine until softened. Add the flour a little at a time, stirring well. Add the milk and cook for 1 minute. Season and add as much stock as required to bring to a soup-like consistency. Remove from heat and cool slightly. Liquidise.

To serve, add chopped parsley, button mushrooms or a swirl of single cream and lashings of warmed wholemeal bread.

SPICY CREOLE ROAST

Serves 6

8 oz (225g) haricot beans, soaked overnight
2 tablespoons oil
2 onions, chopped
1 teaspoon coriander
1 teaspoon cumin
4 oz (125g) mushrooms, sliced
2 carrots, grated
2 sticks celery, finely chopped
1 red pepper, seeded and chopped
2 cloves garlic, chopped
1 fresh chilli, finely chopped
2 tablespoons tomato purée
2 oz (50g) vegetarian Cheddar, grated
4 oz (125g) breadcrumbs
juice of 1/2 lemon
2 oz (50g) chopped nuts
4 oz (125g) canned sweetcorn

a little vegetable stock or watered soy sauce
salt and freshly ground black pepper

FOR THE SAUCE:
1 onion, chopped
2 tablespoons oil
2 carrots, grated
1/2 teaspoon coriander seeds
1/2 pint (275ml) vegetable stock
4 oz (125) canned sweetcorn
dash lemon juice
4 tablespoons fresh orange juice
salt and freshly ground black pepper
fresh parsley to garnish

There seem a lot of expensive ingredients in this loaf, but it is well worth the effort for its colour and flavour. The dish can be made without planning, using canned baked beans.

Drain the beans, cover with fresh water and cook until very soft and mushy (approx. 45 minutes). Heat the oil and fry the vegetables and spices, adding the purée and simmering until tender (about 15 minutes). Stir in the cheese, breadcrumbs, mashed beans, lemon juice, nuts and corn. Season well and add a little stock to form a moist but firm loaf. Bake in a greased 2 lb (900g) loaf tin for 30 minutes at 350F/180C/Gas 4.

To make the sauce, fry the onion in the oil until very soft along with the carrot. Remove from the heat and add all the other ingredients except the parsley. Liquidise until smooth, add the parsley and serve warm, poured over the roast.

TIPSY ORANGE PANCAKES

Serves 4

FOR THE BATTER:
1/2 pint (275ml) milk
1 egg
1 teaspoon oil
4 oz (125g) wholemeal flour

FOR THE FILLING:
2 teaspoons arrowroot
large dash Cointreau or your favourite liqueur
1/4 pint (150ml) fresh orange juice
4 oranges, segmented (or use canned mandarin oranges)
honey, to taste

Greek yoghurt, to serve

Liquidise the batter ingredients until blended. Leave to stand for 1/2 hour.

Make the filling by putting the arrowroot in a pan and gradually mixing in the liquid. Bring to the boil and simmer for 2 minutes until it clears. Add the oranges and reboil. Remove from the heat and add the honey.

Stir the batter and make at least 8 small pancakes in a hot non-stick pan, cooking until both sides are golden brown.

To serve, fill each pancake and fold in half, then in half again. Grated orange zest sprinkled on top looks good and thick Greek yoghurt is the perfect accompaniment.

Judith Rees

I like to take advantage of being so close to the sea and beautiful countryside to take a break from the kitchen to collect ingredients - wild mushrooms, berries and herbs - and inspiration for new dishes and even whole menus; I then can't wait to get back and start cooking again!

CARROT AND LOVAGE SOUP

Serves 4

1 lb (450g) organic carrots
6 oz (175g) potato
6 oz (175g) onion
3/4 pint (400ml) stock
salt and pepper
1/2 pint (275ml) milk, or milk and cream
1 tablespoon lovage
fresh nutmeg

If you can't get hold of lovage you can substitute garlic chives, watercress or coriander leaves.

Clean and coarsely chop the vegetables. Cover with stock and simmer for 20 minutes until tender. Blend until smooth in a food processor. Season with salt and pepper and thin down with the milk.

Finally add a tablespoon of finely chopped lovage leaves and a pinch of freshly grated nutmeg. Heat through for a few minutes to allow the flavours to settle. Serve with poppy seed rolls.

FRESH PASTA WITH WILD MUSHROOMS AND BASIL, WALNUT AND SUN DRIED TOMATO PESTO

Serves 4

FOR THE PESTO:
2 tablespoons basil
2 tablespoons walnuts
2 tablespoons sun dried tomatoes
a little olive oil
1 clove garlic
a little grated Parmesan or vegetarian rennet

FOR THE MUSHROOM SAUCE:
1 onion, finely chopped
2-3 cloves garlic, finely chopped
4 tablespoons good olive oil
1 1/4 lbs (550g) mixed mushrooms eg girolles, ceps, oyster and horse mushrooms
5 fl oz (150ml) dry white wine
salt and black pepper
parsley

12-16 oz (350-450g) fresh pasta

If you have difficulty in obtaining these mushrooms, then use organic chestnut mushrooms, which are more widely available, with a few dried ceps soaked in a little water.

To make the pesto, mix all the ingredients in a food processor. Set aside the sauce until needed.

Gently fry the onion and garlic in the oil without browning for 5-10 minutes. Add the mushrooms.When they begin to soften, pour in the wine and season.

Meanwhile bring a large pan of water to the boil with a few drops of oil in it. Cook the pasta and drain. Pour the mushrooms on top and sprinkle with parsley. Serve with a crisp mixed leaf salad and the pesto.

HAZELNUT MERINGUE WITH BRANDIED APRICOTS

Serves 4-6

4 egg whites
4 oz (125g) light brown sugar
4 oz (125g) icing sugar
4 oz (125g) toasted and ground hazelnuts
6 oz (175g) fresh apricots or dried hunzas, marinated in brandy to taste
8 fl oz (225ml) double cream, thick yoghurt or fromage frais

Whisk the egg whites to soft peaks. Beat in the brown sugar then gently fold in the icing sugar and lastly the hazelnuts. Divide the mixture into 2 x 7 inch (18cm) round cake tins lined with lightly greased foil. Bake for $1^{1}/_{2}$-2 hours at 275F/140C/Gas 1.

When cool, sandwich the meringues with cream, yoghurt or fromage frais and the apricots. Decorate the top in the same way.

Mark Robinson

Cooking skills and vegetarianism came to me while at university. I u as converted from boil-in-the-bag chips and turkey burgers, and taught to cook by my then girlfriend, now wife, Alison. On graduating, Alison worked at Cranks while I learned my skills at the short-lived but influential Christy's Healthline. In 1988 we moved to York to help start The Blake Head. Since Alison left to have our son, I have been Head Chef, though recipes still tend to be jointly developed. Whilst utilising dairy products where necessary, the menus at The Blake Head reflect my own veganism, providing more exciting and wider choice than most vegetarian restaurants for this growing section of customers. The belief that dairy-free food is as joyless as meat-free food was once thought is one we constantly strive to combat with new techniques and new approaches.

PASTA, PESTO AND AVOCADO SALAD

Serves 4

6-8 oz (175-225g) organic white penne pasta
olive oil
4 tomatoes, diced, plus extra to garnish
1-2 avocados, sliced
lollo rosso leaves
black olives

FOR THE PESTO:
2 oz (50g) fresh basil
3 tablespoons pine kernels, toasted
3 cloves garlic, crushed
3-4 fl oz (75-125ml) olive oil
2-3 teaspoons lemon juice
salt and pepper to taste

Cook the pasta in boiling salted water until al dente - soft but with a little bite left. Drain and rinse. Toss in a little olive oil to prevent it sticking together.

While the pasta is cooking, combine the pesto ingredients in a blender until almost, but not quite, smooth. Season to taste. Mix together the pasta, pesto and chopped tomato, keeping aside a few spoonfuls of the pesto dressing.

When ready to serve, arrange the pasta on a plate, garnish with the extra tomato, lollo rosso and olives and arrange thin slices of avocado on top. Spoon the reserved pesto dressing over the avocado and serve.

ITALIAN AUBERGINE AND TOFU LAYER

Serves 4

1 lb (450g) tofu

FOR THE MARINADE:

1 glass red wine
¹/₂ glass cider vinegar
¹/₂ glass shoyu, water to top up
3-4 aubergines
salt, oil

FOR THE TOMATO SAUCE:

3 tablespoons olive oil
2 onions, finely chopped
2 sticks celery, finely chopped
2-3 carrots, finely diced
1 tablespoon basil, 1 teaspoon oregano
1 lb (450g) brown capped mushrooms, thickly sliced
2 lb (900g) tomatoes, diced
2 teaspoons tomato purée
salt and pepper
6 oz (175g) wholewheat breadcrumbs
3 oz (75g) sesame seeds
1 oz (25g) parsley, finely chopped

Cut tofu into slices approximately 3 ins (7.5cm) x 1¹/₂ ins (3.5cm) x ¹/₂ in (1cm) and marinate in the marinade for at least 2-3 hours, preferably overnight.

Slice the aubergines into rings about ¹/₂ in (1cm) thick, sprinkle with salt and leave for 45 minutes. Then rinse well, brush with oil and bake in a pre-heated oven at 375F/190C/Gas 5 until soft.

Spread the marinated tofu out on a tray, brush with olive oil and bake for about 25 minutes. Meanwhile prepare the tomato sauce. Sauté the onions, celery and carrots for 5-10 minutes until soft but not browned; add the herbs, mushrooms, tomatoes and tomato purée and bring to the boil. Reduce the heat and simmer until the sauce is fairly thick. Season to taste with salt and pepper.

Combine the breadcrumbs, sesame seeds and chopped parsley. Layer a large ovenproof dish (or individual dishes) with the tofu, aubergines and tomato sauce, starting and ending with the tomato sauce. Make a final layer with the breadcrumb/sesame mixture. Bake in the oven for about 30-35 minutes until golden brown. Serve with either a crisp green salad or seasonal vegetables.

TROPICAL FRUIT
TERRINE

Serves 4

8 passion fruits
1 1/4 pints (700ml) pineapple juice
5 fl oz (150ml) white wine
5 oz (150g) soft light brown sugar
2-3 oz (50-75g) agar agar
strawberries
kiwi fruit

Halve each passion fruit and scoop out the middle using a melon baller. Add this to the pineapple juice, sugar and white wine in a pan and bring to the boil. Cook for 2 minutes, then strain the mixture into a measuring jug, discarding the pips.

Take note of the amount of liquid – it should be about $1\frac{1}{2}$ pints (900ml). Return the liquid to the pan, bring to the boil and add the agar agar as instructed on the packet – the amount needed and method sometimes varies. Stir thoroughly and add to the remaining fruit mixture, straining again if desired. Refrigerate while you prepare the dishes.

Slice the strawberries and kiwi fruits. Take 4 timbales or dessert dishes and place the kiwi fruit in the bottom and the strawberries around the sides. Doing this carefully makes all the difference!

When the juice mixture has cooled down and is starting to thicken but before it is set, pour it gently into the lined dishes. Refrigerate for at least 2 hours and turn the terrines out just before serving, inverting them gently on to the plate. Excellent served with a syrup infused with lime juice, or to accompany a fresh fruit salad.

Jane Stimpson, Angela Gamble, Mariola Goldsmith

FOOD FOR THOUGHT · LONDON WC2

Jane Stimpson

Frustrated by the repetitiveness of production-line cooking, I have been a chef at Food for Thought since 1986 and am particularly attracted to the spices and seasonings of the East which I use to give added interest to simple vegetables.

Angela Gamble

Instead of following an unhappy destiny in banking, I made an impulsive decision to join a team of vegetarian chefs and, six years later, am still loving it! I now make full use of the freedom to experiment, and have discovered unsuspected creative talents.

Mariola Goldsmith

Coming from Poland before the fall of Communism, I discovered my cooking talents at Food for Thought when I was finally freed from the tyranny of cleaning ovens by the positive encouragement of my boss. Now I dreams the next day's menus and trusts to my hands to fulfil the night's vision!

MISO AND NORI SOUP

Serves 4-6

FOR THE MUSHROOM STOCK:
1/2 teaspoon black peppercorns
1 small onion, halved and stuck with 1 clove
1 celery top and tail piece
4-5 carrot tops or 1 carrot, sliced
1 parsnip (optional)
4 oz (125g) mushroom stalks

4 parsley stalks or 1 sprig parsley
1 bay leaf
1 1/2 pints (900ml) cold water

1 medium onion, finely sliced
1 dessertspoon soya or vegetable oil
1 clove garlic, crushed
1 teaspoon grated root ginger
pinch chilli powder if liked
1 carrot, sliced into julienne strips
1 dessertspoon tomato purée
1 dessertspoon miso

2 sheets nori seaweed
2 oz (50g) mushrooms, sliced (dried Chinese
mushrooms give a very good flavour)
1 bunch spring onions, sliced
1 tablespoon peas
6 baby corn, cut slantwise into thirds
1 small tin bamboo shoots (optional)
1 tablespoon chopped fresh coriander
1 glass sweet or medium dry sherry
tamari or soy sauce, to season
1-2 teaspoons apple juice concentrate or honey, to
taste

*If you are short of time, use a vegetable stock cube
instead of the mushroom stock.*

Bring all ingredients for the mushroom stock to
the boil and simmer for 1 hour (or 20 minutes
in the pressure cooker). Set aside.

Fry the onion in the oil until soft. Add the
garlic, root ginger and chilli if liked. Stir-fry for
1 minute. Add the carrot julienne and stir-fry
for another minute. Add the tomato purée and
miso and continue to stir-fry briefly. Add a
little stock if the mixture is too dry, to prevent
sticking. Remove from the heat.

Lightly toast the nori, either by waving the
sheets through a gas flame 3 or 4 times or by
placing under the grill for 1 minute. Tear the
nori into thin strips.

Pour the strained,reserved mushroom stock
over the stir-fry mixture, add the nori and once
boiling, add the remaining vegetables (reserve
a handful of mushrooms, spring onions and
coriander for the final garnish).

SPINACH AND SHIITAKE FILO PIE

Serves 6

2 medium onions, finely chopped
2 bunches spring onions, finely chopped
4 sticks celery, finely chopped
1 oz (25g) butter
2 cloves garlic
fresh thyme
2 lbs (900g) spinach
pinch nutmeg
salt and pepper
3 free range eggs
2 full dessertspoons Greek yoghurt
fresh basil
8 oz (225g) feta cheese
tabasco sauce, to taste
8 oz (225g) shiitake or oyster mushrooms, sliced
soya sauce to taste
14 oz (400g) filo pastry
chopped fresh herbs, eg dill, chives, basil
(optional)

*This easily-prepared light summer dish may be
served with a mixed leaf salad or asparagus, mange-
tout and baby corn. Shiitake mushrooms have a
chewy, fibrous, 'meaty' taste and are available in
most large supermarkets; fresh oyster mushrooms
may be substituted.*

Fry the onions, 1 bunch of spring onions and
celery gently in the butter with 1 crushed clove
of garlic and a little fresh thyme until softened.
Wash the spinach very thoroughly (2 or 3
rinses) and drain. Blanch the spinach until the
leaves are just limp, with nutmeg, salt and
pepper. Drain in a colander.

Blend the onion mixture with the spinach to
the preferred consistency, or chop it up finely
with a sharp knife. Add the beaten eggs,

yoghurt and chopped fresh basil, and mix. Stir in the remaining bunch of chopped spring onions, cubed feta cheese and a dash of tabasco.

Stir-fry the sliced mushrooms with the remaining garlic and a dash of soya sauce, then drain. Lightly grease a pie dish and use $1/2$ the packet of filo pastry to line the base, lightly brushing each layer with melted butter. Spoon the spinach mixture into the lined pie dish, layer the mushroom slices on top of the spinach and top with the remaining filo pastry - add fresh herbs between the last few layers of filo for an attractive finish. Score the top into diamonds with a sharp knife.

Cook in an oven pre-heated to 325F/170C/Gas 3 for 10 minutes, then cover with foil to prevent scorching, and continue to cook for a further 20 minutes. Leave to stand for 5 minutes before serving hot, or alternatively serve cold.

SUMMER DREAM PATISSIERE

Serves 4-6

FOR THE BASE:
1½ rounded tablespoons ground walnuts or almonds
1 dessertspoon sugar
6 oz (175g) flour
3 oz (75g) margarine or butter
a little milk to bind

FOR THE CREME PATISSIERE:
½ pint (275ml) milk, steeped with a vanilla pod
2 tablespoons custard powder
2 teaspoons sugar
1 tablespoon cream

FOR THE SAUCE:
1 lb (450g) strawberries or raspberries, chopped
2 tablespoons sherry
3 teaspoons sugar
zest of 1 lemon

8 oz (225g) strawberries, 1 kiwi fruit, walnut halves or flaked almonds, to decorate

Mix the dry ingredients, then rub in the fat until the mixture resembles fine crumbs. Add a little milk to bind. Roll or press out into an 8 inch (20.5cm) round baking tray or flan ring and bake for 15 minutes in a hot oven until golden. Chill.

Warm the milk with the vanilla pod but do not allow to boil. Leave for $1/2$ hour to allow the flavour to infuse. Blend the custard powder with a little of the milk to a smooth cream. Pour in the rest of the milk gradually, blending thoroughly. Return to the heat, bring to the boil for 3 minutes and then stir in the cream off the heat. Pour over the base, still in its baking tin, and chill.

In a heavy pan, simmer the fruit very slowly till soft with the other ingredients for the sauce. Add a little water or apple juice to prevent sticking. Blend very thoroughly. If you don't like seeds, strain through a very fine sieve. Pour over the base and chill.

Cut the strawberries in half but do not hull as the green leaves look very pretty. Peel and slice the kiwi and alternate with strawberries on the topping. Place the walnuts or almonds (depending on the base) attractively between the fruit slices. Serve and enjoy with a chilled glass of Beaumes de Venise.

David Scott and P.J. Byrne

E V E R Y M A N   B I S T R O   ·   L I V E R P O O L

The Bistro has been established here for twenty-one years with the basic aim of feeding people who live, work and play in the area with good, interesting food; a great many people eat here five times a week. With the exception of tomatoes and a few other items, no tinned or frozen foods or additives are used. Vegetables arrive fresh from the market every morning. Local sources are used wherever possible; for example, Lancashire cheese comes from Mrs Kirkham's 39 cows and Cheshire from Appleby's of Hawkstone, the last remaining traditional cheese maker in the county.

The menu changes twice a day and although there are many regular dishes, the selection is very much affected by the season and what is available from the markets that day, reflecting cosmopolitan Liverpool as well as rural Lancashire and Cheshire. Dishes are produced in small batches (a maximum of 24 portions). As many as 16 savoury specials (perhaps 50% vegetarian) and the same number of special desserts may be cooked during the course of the day.

PEAR AND AVOCADO SALAD WITH TAHINI MAYONNAISE

Serves 4

3 teaspoons tahini paste
3 tablespoons mayonnaise
1 medium ripe avocado
1 ripe pear
2 limes
chicory to garnish

Combine the tahini and mayonnaise and mix well together. Peel the pear and avocado. Cut each into halves or quarters lengthways and remove the core and stone. Cut these halves or quarters lengthways into fairly thin slices. Divide between 4 plates, making a fan shape of alternate slices of avocado and pear. At the base of the 'fan', place a tablespoon (15ml) of the tahini mayonnaise.

Slice one of the limes and arrange as a garnish with the chicory leaves. Squeeze the juice of the second lime over the pear and avocado arrangements and serve.

Recipe taken from 'The Penniless Vegetarian'
© David Scott

STUFFED COURGETTES
WITH APRICOTS

Serves 4

4 medium courgettes, sliced lengthways
3 tablespoons olive oil
1 medium onion, diced
8 oz (225g) long grain rice
1 tablespoon tomato purée
½ teaspoon sugar
1 teaspoon ground cinnamon
salt and black pepper
1 tablespoon honey
8 oz (225g) dried apricots, diced
juice of 1 lemon

Scoop the pulp out of the courgettes, leaving the shells about ¾ inch (2cm) thick. Chop up the scooped out pulp. Heat the oil in a heavy pan, add the onion and courgette pulp and sauté until the onion is just soft. Add the rice, 8 fl oz (225ml) water, tomato purée, sugar, cinnamon and salt and black pepper to taste. Bring to the boil, reduce to simmer and cook for 15 minutes with occasional stirring.

Meanwhile cover the courgette shells in boiling salted water and leave for 2-3 minutes. Drain them, stuff with the rice mixture and set aside. Combine 16 fl oz (450ml) water with the honey and apricots and boil until the apricots are completely softened. Preheat the oven to 350F/180C/Gas 4. Spoon into a heavy casserole dish half the apricots and their juice, place the stuffed courgettes on top and pour over the remaining apricots and juice. Sprinkle with the lemon juice and bake for 30 minutes or until the courgettes are just soft and tender. Serve hot or cold.

Recipe taken from 'The Penniless Vegetarian'
© David Scott

ORIENTAL FRUIT SALAD

Serves 4

10 dried figs, cut into uneven pieces
10 fresh or dried dates, stoned and cut into quarters or pieces
2 oz (50g) whole, unskinned almonds
2 oz (50g) whole, unskinned hazelnuts
4 tablespoons kirsch
1 small honeydew or Ogen melon, peeled, sliced and cubed
14 oz (400g) tinned pineapple chunks in unsweetened juice

Mix the figs, dates and nuts together. Pour over the kirsch, cover and leave to marinate for several hours (preferably overnight). Mix the melon and pineapple chunks with the steeped fruit and nuts and pour over the juice from the pineapple. Put the salad into an attractive bowl and chill before serving.

Recipe taken from 'Simply Vegan'
© David Scott

Dorothy Smith

LUPTON TOWER · KIRKBY LONSDALE

Lupton Tower is a charming eighteenth century house with gardens looking across pastureland to Farleton Fell. We are a vegetarian guest house and restaurant and we place particular emphasis on the use of fresh fruits and vegetables; individual timbales, mousses and soufflés are a speciality. I like to make my own bread, ice creams and sorbets and even dabble in a little cheese making.

SPINACH MOUSSELINE WITH YOGHURT AND DILL SAUCE

Serves 4

3 lbs (1.4kg) spinach
4 shallots
butter
8 oz (225g) low fat cream cheese
2 eggs, separated
1 oz (25g) butter
grated nutmeg
salt and pepper
lemon wedges and sprigs of dill, to decorate

FOR THE YOGHURT AND DILL SAUCE:
1/2 pint (275ml) natural yoghurt
2 tablespoons chopped fresh dill
juice of 1/2 lemon
pinch caster sugar

Trim the stalks off the spinach and wash well. Cook in a very small amount of water until tender, then drain out as much of the liquid as possible. Sauté the shallots in butter until tender, add the spinach and combine.

Put the spinach mixture, cream cheese, egg yolks and seasoning in a food processor and blend. Whip the egg whites until stiff and fold into the blended mixture. Grease 4 x 5 fl oz (150ml) ramekins and fill with the mixture. Cook in a bain-marie for 25 minutes. Leave to stand for 5 minutes before turning out. Decorate with lemon wedges and sprigs of dill.

Combine all the ingredients for the sauce together and serve with the mousseline.

CHESTNUT AND FIG ROLL WITH CUMBERLAND SAUCE

Serves 4

1 onion, finely chopped
2 sticks celery, finely chopped
1 oz (25g) butter, plus extra for covering greaseproof paper
2 small bread rolls, soaked in milk for 2 hours
1 tablespoon fresh mixed herbs
4 oz (125g) chestnuts (if dried soak overnight and

cook for 1/2 hour or more)
4 oz (125g) dried figs, chopped
2 eggs
1 spring cabbage

1 orange
1 lemon
2 teaspoons arrowroot
1 teaspoon Dijon mustard
6 tablespoons redcurrant jelly
3 tablespoons port

Fry the onion and celery gently in butter until tender. Squeeze the excess milk out of the bread rolls and break them up. Add these to the onion mixture along with the herbs, chestnuts and figs. Take off the heat and combine with the eggs to create a moist, but not wet, mixture. Add a few breadcrumbs if the mixture is too wet.

Take the central core out of the cabbage, separate the leaves, blanch in boiling water for 2-3 minutes and drain on kitchen paper.

Take a large sheet of tin foil and place a sheet of greaseproof paper on top. Cover all over with butter and place the cabbage leaves on the greaseproof paper. Mould the chestnut mixture into a roll, place in the centre of the cabbage leaves and roll up using the tin foil. Seal the tin foil (not too tightly, to allow for expansion), place on a rack over a roasting tin filled with water and bake for approx. 1 hour at 350F/180C/Gas 4. Leave to cool for 5-10 minutes before slicing and serving on the sauce.

To make the sauce, cut the zest from the orange into matchstick lengths and simmer gently in 1/2 pint (275ml) water for 10 minutes. Squeeze the juice from the orange and lemon and mix with the arrowroot and mustard.

Combine them in the pan together with the redcurrant jelly and port. Bring to the boil, then simmer until the sauce becomes clear.

APPLE AND CALVADOS SYLLABUB WITH ALMOND SHORTBREAD

Serves 4

1 lb (450g) Granny Smith's apples
1/2 pint (275ml) double or whipping cream
4 fl oz (125ml) white wine
4 fl oz (125ml) Calvados
2 oz (50g) caster sugar
juice and zest of 1/2 lemon
mint sprigs and apple slices, to decorate

FOR ALMOND SHORTBREAD·
5 oz (150g) plain flour
5 oz (150g) butter
2 1/2 oz (65g) cornflour
2 1/2 oz (65g) caster sugar
1/2 teaspoon almond essence

Peel, core and quarter the apples, cook until tender, then purée. Whip the cream slowly, adding the white wine, Calvados, sugar and lemon; the mixture should reach the soft peak stage only. Gently fold in the apple purée and pour into glasses.

Combine all the ingredients for the shortbread in a food processor. Roll out quite thinly and cut into the desired shapes with a pastry cutter. Place on a baking sheet and bake for approx. 20 minutes at 325F/170C/Gas 3. Serve the syllabub accompanied by the almond shortbread and decorated with mint sprigs and apple slices.

Jenny Urbanowicz

THYMES · BIDEFORD

The restaurant is housed within an 18th century bakehouse, for many years sitting derelict, until I felt that the sad lack of good vegetarian cuisine in the town should be corrected! Having run Thymes successfully for over six years now, we have built up a loyal local clientele. As we are situated in one of Bideford's narrow winding streets, visitors often discover the extensive vegetarian menu quite by accident, and are always eager to return to sample more homemade treats. Daily specials are cooked early each morning to ensure that nothing but freshly prepared, wholesome food is served up from our open-plan kitchen.

THYMES SOUP

Serves 4-6

¹/₂ onion, chopped
¹/₂ stick celery, chopped
¹/₄ swede, diced, ¹/₂ parsnip, diced
4 or 5 large carrots, diced
few cauliflower florets
3 leeks, chopped
sunflower or soya oil
8-10 oz (225-275g) red lentils or yellow split peas
2 teaspoons dried or fresh mixed herbs
1 very large tablespoon Vecon (the best vegetable stock, available from health food shops)
generous dash soya sauce
1 or 2 bay leaves

Sauté all the vegetables in oil for approx. 5 minutes. Then add the lentils or split peas, mixed herbs, Vecon, soya sauce and bay leaves. Mix well and add water to top up the pan. Bring to the boil, then simmer, adding more water as necessary.

LENTIL AND POTATO BAKE

Serves 4-5

1 onion
2 cloves garlic
¹/₂ stick celery
3 carrots, sliced lengthways
¹/₂ cauliflower
8 oz (225g) courgettes
1 lb (450g) leeks
1 dried chilli, chopped small
sunflower oil
8 oz (225g) frozen sliced beans (optional)
1 large tin tomatoes
¹/₃ tube tomato purée
scant tablespoon Vecon
3 tablespoons soya sauce
1 tablespoon paprika
1 teaspoon dried or fresh rosemary
3 lbs (1.4kg) potatoes, cooked and mashed with margarine, milk, black pepper and salt
6-8 oz (175-225g) red lentils

Chop the first 7 vegetables and put into a large saucepan with the chilli and a little oil. Cover and sweat very gently on a low heat for about 20 minutes until the vegetables are cooked but not mushy. Add the beans, tin of tomatoes, tomato purée, Vecon, soya sauce, paprika and rosemary. Cook for approx. 20 minutes until everything is well blended.

Cook the red lentils, mix with the vegetables and transfer to a shallow ovenproof dish. Spread the mashed potato over the vegetables and lentils and cook in the oven for 45 minutes at 325F/170C/Gas 3-4.

PEAR AND ALMOND TART

Serves 6-7

pastry case, made with wholemeal flour, to line 8$^1/_2$ inch (21.5cm) tin

2 tablespoons apricot jam
2 medium fresh pears (do not peel)
4 oz (125g) margarine
4 oz (125g) soft brown sugar
2 eggs
4 oz (125g) ground almonds
2 oz (50g) plain flour
2 capfuls natural vanilla essence

Par-bake the pastry case for 5 minutes. Chop the pears into smallish pieces and mix with the apricot jam. Line the pastry case with the mixture.

Mix all the other ingredients together and beat well for 5 minutes. Spread this mixture over the pears and jam and cook in the oven for 20-30 minutes at 325F/170C/Gas 3-4 until golden brown.

Colin and Louisa Le Voi

The Quince and Medlar was already an established and popular vegetarian restaurant with many regular customers when we took it over; we felt we must honour its present standing and oblige the obvious need for good vegetarian food. Colin's training had been traditional, latterly at Sharrow Bay, Ullswater, where the fare was far from vegetarian but the valued experience there and a good deal of research into vegetarian philosophy was excellent equipment for the formidable challenge of our first restaurateur/owner venture. We live on the premises and think of customers as guests in our home where special attention is given to the details which make eating out memorable. Nutritional balance is the aim, as well as good presentation and delighting the palate. The challenge has brought us, and hopefully our customers, great satisfaction, particularly as we were awarded in 1989, our first year, the Vegetarian Society's Best Vegetarian Restaurant of the Year Award, an honour which was repeated for 1991.

TERRINE OF YOUNG VEGETABLES WITH PINE KERNELS

Serves 6

1½ lbs (700g) spinach (blanched and drained)
1 tablespoon chopped parsley
1 tablespoon chopped chives
5 fl oz (150ml) double cream
3 eggs
3 oz (75g) young leeks
3 oz (75g) baby carrots
3 oz (75g) young corn
3 oz (75g) red pepper
3 oz (75g) asparagus
2 oz (50g) toasted pine kernels
salt and pepper
grated nutmeg

Place the spinach, herbs, cream and eggs in a food processor and blend until smooth. Season to taste. Prepare the vegetables and cut the red pepper into strips - blanch separately in salted water until tender and drain well.

Line a 2¼ pint (1.3 litre) terrine with buttered greaseproof paper and layer the spinach mixture with the vegetables and toasted pine kernels in alternate layers, finishing with the spinach.

Cover with buttered greaseproof paper and cook in a bain-marie at 350F/180C/Gas 4 for 1-1½ hours or until set. Allow to cool thoroughly before turning out of terrine tin. Cut into slices and serve chilled with a sauce of your choice.

SMOKED CHEESE ROULADE WITH MUSHROOM PÂTÉ

Serves 4

FOR THE ROULADE:
2 oz (50g) butter
2 oz (50g) cornflour
1/2 pint (275ml) milk
8 oz (225g) smoked Westmorland cheese, grated
4 eggs, separated
1/2 teaspoon salt
1/2 teaspoon cayenne pepper

FOR THE PÂTÉ:
1 large onion
2 oz (50g) butter
1 1/2 lbs (700g) mushrooms
4 fl oz (125ml) red wine

Preheat the oven to 350F/180C/Gas 4. Melt the butter in a heavy-bottomed pan, add the cornflour and mix thoroughly. Slowly pour in the milk and stir vigorously until the mixture forms a ball. Place in a food processor and add the cheese, egg yolks and seasoning. Blend. Using a balloon whisk, beat the egg whites in a clean, dry bowl until stiff. Gently fold the cheesy mixture into the egg whites. Line a Swiss roll tin with greaseproof paper and fill with the mixture. Bake for 20 minutes.

To make the pâté, finely chop the onion and sauté in butter. Finely chop the mushrooms and add to the pan. Cook for another minute. Add the red wine and simmer for 20 minutes or until the wine and mushrooms have reduced to pâté consistency. Turn out the baked roulade on to a large sheet of greaseproof paper. Evenly spread the pâté over it. Gently roll up from one of the long ends like a Swiss roll. Serve in slices.

CHOCOLATE ORANGE PIE

Serves 7-8

4 fl oz (125ml) liquid glucose
juice and zest of 2 oranges
3 oz (75g) sugar
1 lb (450g) plain chocolate
4 tablespoons Cointreau
15 fl oz (400ml) double cream

Line a loose-bottomed 10 inch (25cm) round tin with clingfilm.

Place the glucose, orange juice and zest and sugar in a pan - heat gently to melt the sugar then bring to the boil.

Gently melt the chocolate with the liqueur. Combine the glucose mixture with the chocolate mixture and leave to cool.

Beat the cream to soft peaks then fold into the cooled chocolate mixture. Turn the mixture into the tin and chill for at least 8 hours. Serve with whipped cream.

Sue Wild

THE GOOD EARTH · WELLS

The Good Earth was opened in the 70's and purchased from the original owners in 1983. Formerly a hotel called 'The Antelope', it is now an 80 cover restaurant with an adjacent wholefood store; we serve totally vegetarian meals which include an increasing quantitiy of organic products.

CREAM OF PARSNIP AND APPLE SOUP

Serves 6

2 oz (50g) butter or margarine
1 large onion, chopped
1 lb (450g) parsnips, peeled and sliced
2 large cooking apples, peeled and sliced
1 pint (570ml) water or vegetable stock
salt and pepper
milk
cream (optional)

Melt the butter in a large pan and fry the onions, parsnips and apples for 5-10 minutes.

Add the water or stock, and seasoning, and simmer for another 15-20 minutes or until the parsnips are soft. Purée the soup in a blender and return to the pan.

Add milk and cream to the required consistency, adjust the seasoning and heat through.

PASTA WITH MUSHROOMS AND THREE CHEESES

Serves 6

1 oz (25g) butter or margarine
1 large onion, chopped, 1 clove garlic, crushed
8 oz (225g) mushrooms, sliced
1 oz (25g) flour, 1 pint (570ml) milk
2 oz (50g) Brie, rind removed and sliced
2 oz (50g) Stilton, crumbled
2 oz (50g) Cheddar, grated
salt and pepper
10-12 oz (275-350g) pasta shapes

Melt the butter in a large pan, add the onion and garlic and fry for 2 minutes. Add the mushrooms and fry for a further minute. Remove the pan from the heat and stir in the flour. Return to the heat and gradually stir in the milk.

When the sauce has boiled and thickened, add the Brie, Stilton and half the Cheddar and stir until the cheese has melted. Season to taste.

Cook the pasta in boiling, salted water. Drain and rinse the pasta and place in the bottom of an ovenproof dish. Pour the mushroom sauce over the pasta and sprinkle with the remaining Cheddar cheese. Brown under a hot grill.

TOFFEE APPLE PUDDING

Serves 6

½ pint (275ml) whipping cream
1 oz (25g) butter or margarine
12 oz (350g) soft brown sugar
½ teaspoon vanilla essence
6 oz (175g) margarine
3 eggs
6 oz (175g) self-raising flour
3 large cooking apples, peeled and sliced

Heat the oven to 375F/190C/Gas 5. Combine the cream, butter and 6 oz (175g) of the sugar together in a pan. Bring slowly to the boil, stirring occasionally. Boil rapidly for 5 minutes, then add the vanilla essence.

Beat the rest of the sugar with the margarine until light and fluffy. Add the eggs and flour and beat well.

Pour enough sauce into an ovenproof dish to cover the bottom. Arrange half the apple slices in the sauce. Cover the apples with half the sponge mixture, then another layer of apples and the rest of the sponge.

Cook in the oven for 30-45 minutes or until the sponge is firm to the touch. Turn the pudding upside down on to a plate and pour the rest of the sauce over the top. Serve hot with cream or custard.

Hilda Wright

The Redesdale Arms, for many years locally known as 'The First and Last' as it used to be the first or last hotel in England, is an old coaching inn only 12 miles from the England/Scotland border. Situated in the beautiful Rede Valley, it is on the edge of the giant Redesdale/Kielder forest complex. We have a separate vegetarian menu based on the very best local seasonal vegetables, offering the choice of both good country food and more exotic specialities.

PEACHES STUFFED WITH CREAM CHEESE AND WALNUTS

Serves 4

4 fresh peaches
8 oz (225g) cream cheese
4 oz (125g) walnuts
½ iceberg lettuce

Cut the peaches in half and remove the stone. Chop the walnuts, combine with the cream cheese and use to fill the peaches. Shred the iceberg lettuce and serve the peaches on a bed of the lettuce with a suitable garnish.

BEAN AND CIDER CASSEROLE

Serves 4

2 tablespoons vegetable oil
2 medium onions, sliced
2 cloves garlic, crushed
1 medium green pepper, diced
2 medium courgettes, sliced
1 bayleaf
2 tablespoons tomato purée
8 oz (225g) cooked kidney beans
8 fl oz (225ml) dry cider

It is most important that the kidney beans are thoroughly cooked before being used in this recipe.

Set the oven to 375F/190C/Gas 5. Heat the oil in a heavy pan and sauté the onions and garlic. Add the green pepper and courgettes, stir and gently sauté until soft. Pour the mixture into a casserole dish, add the remaining ingredients and bake for 40 minutes. Serve with baked potatoes, carrots and broccoli.

HOT CHOCOLATE
FUDGE CAKE

Makes 2 large cakes

2 ¹/₄ lbs (1kg) self-raising flour, to include
9 dessertspoons cocoa powder
9 teaspoons baking powder
2 ¹/₄ lbs (1kg) margarine
2 ¹/₄ lbs (1kg) sugar
18 eggs

FOR THE TOPPING:
12 oz (350g) granulated sugar
1 tin evaporated milk
1 lb (450g) cooking chocolate
6 oz (175g) margarine
8 drops vanilla essence

*This makes a large quantity, but both cakes and
topping will freeze.*

Mix all the ingredients for the cake together,
pour into 2 large, flat baking trays and cook in
a medium oven (350-375F/180-190C/Gas 4-5)
for 1 hour.

Heat the sugar and milk. Boil for 6 minutes
without stirring. Turn off the heat, add the
chocolate, margarine and vanilla essence.
Allow to cool for 2 hours and spread over the
cakes.

Amanda Wingrove

BYRAMS BISTRO · HUDDERSFIELD

Situated in the heart of Huddersfield, Byrams is a family-run bistro which prides itself on freshly prepared dishes served in a relaxed and friendly atmosphere. The restaurant is open in the morning for coffee and croissants or sandwiches and there is always a vegetarian selection on the lunch and dinner menus. Our chefs experiment with flavours, colours and presentation of each vegetarian dish before it goes on to the menu - we have a reputation for providing the most original selection for vegetarians in the area.

GAUFRES DE LEGUMES, SAUCE SOUBISE

Serves 4

FOR THE FILLING:
2 oz (50g) butter
2 medium carrots, diced
1 medium onion, diced
2 cloves garlic, chopped
2 courgettes, sliced
3 oz (75g) cabbage, shredded
1 lb (450g) chopped cooked tomatoes
1 tablespoon tomato purée
salt and ground black pepper to taste
1 small glass white wine
3 oz (75g) beansprouts

FOR THE SAUCE:
2 oz (50g) butter
1 medium onion, diced
2 oz (50g) flour
$\frac{1}{2}$ pint (275ml) milk
salt and ground black pepper to taste

8 oz (225g) filo pastry
2 oz (50g) butter
chopped parsley and cayenne pepper, to garnish

Melt the butter and gently sweat off the diced carrots, onion and garlic, then add the sliced courgettes, shredded cabbage, chopped tomatoes and tomato purée. Check for seasoning and add the wine. When all the vegetables are virtually cooked, add the beansprouts and leave the mixture to cool.

To make the sauce, gently melt the butter in a thick-bottomed pan; sweat off the diced onion to soften, but do not colour. Then add the flour and make a roux. Gradually add the milk and check for seasoning.

Cut the filo pastry into 6 ins x 3 ins (15cm x 7cm) strips. Melt the butter and use it to brush a large baking tray. Place two pastry strips per person on the tray (8 for 4 people). Butter the pastry strips and build each one up to 3 layers, making sure you butter each layer. Fill the centre of each with the filling, then cover with another 3 layers of buttered pastry. Cook for approx. 15 minutes in a moderate oven until golden brown.

Place 2 gaufres per person on a hot plate and serve with the hot soubise sauce poured between them. Sprinkle with chopped parsley and cayenne pepper.

AUBERGINE ET OIGNONS FRITS PROVENCALE

Serves 4

FOR THE SAUCE:
3 oz (75g) chopped onion
1 clove garlic
1 oz (25g) butter
1 tablespoon tomato puree
1 small glass white wine
1 lb (450g) diced tinned tomatoes
salt and black pepper to taste
pinch tarragon
Tabasco sauce, to taste
3 oz (75g) sliced mushrooms
FOR THE BATTER:
1 egg
3 oz (75g) plain flour
7 fl oz (200ml) water
1/2 teaspoon cayenne pepper
salt and pepper
drop of vinegar
drop of Tabasco
1 aubergine
1 onion
oil for frying
chopped parsley, to garnish

Sweat off the onions and garlic in the butter until soft but not coloured. Add the tomato purée, wine, tinned tomatoes, salt and pepper, tarragon and Tabasco. Simmer gently for approx. 10 minutes, then add the mushrooms and simmer for another 5 minutes. Check for seasoning; the sauce should be hot and spicy.

To make the batter, mix the beaten egg with the flour and let down to a thick coating consistency with the water. Add all the seasoning and beat well; leave to stand for a while.

Slice the aubergine into 1/4 inch (0.5cm) slices. Slice the onion, not too thinly, and separate into rings. Dip the aubergine slices and onion rings into flour and then into the batter. Deep fry in hot oil (300F/160C) until golden brown. Serve the onion rings and aubergine slices alternately in a dish and garnish with chopped parsley. Serve the Provencale sauce in a separate sauce boat.

FRAISES WILHELMINE

Serves 4

1½ lbs (700g) fresh strawberries
5 fl oz (150ml) fresh orange juice
4 oz (125g) caster sugar
kirsch, to taste
whipped double cream, to garnish
vanilla essence

Save 4 strawberries to garnish and then liquidise the strawberries, orange juice and caster sugar. Add kirsch to taste. Place the mixture in glass dishes and chill well. Garnish with the whipped cream flavoured with vanilla esence and a little caster sugar if you wish. Place a whole or fanned strawberry in the centre of the dish and serve straight from the refrigerator.

Mike Wood

Woody's is situated in the picturesque Pennine village of Delph, Saddleworth, near Oldham. This is an ideal restaurant for those tired of the 'scrubbed pine and sackcloth' image of vegetarianism. We have put much thought into the creation of an elegant ambience as well as a varied menu which includes two or three vegan dishes and a fine selection of over 70 wines, several of which are organic.

CARROT AND APRICOT PÂTÉ

Serves 5

1 lb (450g) carrots
½ cup dried apricots
2 cloves garlic, crushed
2 oz (50g) Cheddar cheese, grated
10 oz (275g) cottage cheese, sieved
2 eggs, beaten

Cook the carrots and apricots together until soft and purée with the garlic. Add the two cheeses and beaten eggs and place the mixture in a greased and lined loaf tin.

Cook at 400F/200C/Gas 6 for approx. 45 minutes. When cold, cut into slices and serve 2 slices per person with triangles of wholemeal toast.

COURGETTE AND MANGE-TOUT STRUDEL WITH A SWEET AND SOUR SAUCE

Serves 4

8 oz (225g) mange-tout
4 medium courgettes
oil
4 large sheets filo pastry
1 tub goat's cheese, soft variety
pinch nutmeg

FOR THE SWEET AND SOUR SAUCE:
½ pint (275ml) orange or pineapple juice
4 teaspoons soy sauce
2 tablespoons white wine vinegar
2 tablespoons tomato purée
1 oz (25g) brown sugar or honey
arrowroot, to thicken

Top and tail the mange-tout and thinly slice the courgettes. Brush the filo pastry sheets with oil and place on top of each other. Spread with the cheese and top with the vegetables and nutmeg, roll up and cut into 3 or 4. Brush oil on top of the strudels to prevent them drying up and cracking. Cook on a high heat for about 10 minutes. The strudels may be frozen before cooking.

Blend together the ingredients for the sauce, heat and adjust to taste. Thicken with arrowroot.

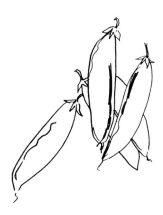

BANANARAMA

Serves 8

FOR THE BASE:
3¹/₂ oz (100g) cream crackers
1 oz (25g) margarine
³/₄ oz (15g) brown sugar
1 oz (25g) coconut
pinch cinnamon

FOR THE TOPPING:
1 pint (570ml) whipping cream
8 oz (225g) golden syrup
4 bananas
extra banana and toasted almonds, to decorate

Combine all the ingredients for the base in a blender and press firmly into a greased cake tin to a depth of about ¹/₄ inch (0.5cm). Bake at 375F/190C/Gas 5 for 5-8 minutes. Stand to cool.

Whisk the cream until thick and mash the bananas and syrup until smooth. Fold in the cream and spoon over the top of the base. Freeze, then divide into portions and keep frozen. When ready to serve, top with toasted almonds and sliced banana.

Kevin Woods

ABBEY GREEN RESTAURANT · CHESTER

Abbey Green Restaurant was founded in 1984 by brother and sister Duncan and Julia Lochhead: Abbey Green was conceived as an answer to a sorely-felt need amongst vegetarians who wanted to eat out in a proper restaurant without having to eat meat or suffer dreadful approximations of vegetarian fare from conventional restaurants. At that time it was almost impossible to find vegetarian restaurants with a decent wine list, comfortable furnishings, haute cuisine cooking or classical music, many of the things that 'omnivores' take for granted, as the vegetarian eating-out culture at that time centred around alternative youth cafes, most of which weren't open in the evenings anyway. From the beginning we tried as far as possible to write our own recipes, and to get away from the perceived wholefoody stodginess of vegetarian cooking. Things have changed: we have been in the Good Food Guide for six years, we were awarded the Vegetarian Society's Vegetarian Restaurant of the Year in 1988, and in 1990 we were the Good Food Guide's County Restaurant of the year, which included all the meat restaurants, so we are now perceived as being almost part of normal life!

═══════════════

SWEETCORN, ARTICHOKE AND CASHEW NUT FRICASSEE IN A PARMESAN RING

Serves 4

FOR THE GOUGERE:
3 oz (75g) butter
5 fl oz (150ml) water
pinch salt
2 oz (50g) flour
1 tablespoon freshly grated Parmesan
3 eggs

FOR THE FRICASSEE:
1 onion, diced
1 clove garlic, crushed
1 fl oz (25ml) olive oil
14 oz (400g) peeled artichokes, diced
2 oz (50g) flour
1 pint (570ml) vegetable stock
14 oz (400g) baby sweetcorn
7 oz (200g) chopped roasted cashews
1/2 pint (275ml) double cream
5 fl oz (150ml) sherry or muscat wine
fresh dill, to decorate

To make the gougere ring, melt the butter in a saucepan with the water and salt and simmer for 2 minutes. Add the flour and Parmesan, stir and cook until the dough leaves the sides of the pan. Put immediately into a blender and blend with 3 whole eggs - it is then ready to pipe into 4 x 5 inch (12.5cm) ring shapes on to a baking sheet. Cook on 350F/180C/Gas 4 for 15 minutes then turn down to 275F/140C/Gas 1 for approx. 5-10 minutes until the rings are brown and dry.

Cooked as a fricassee, this dish manages to keep the individual flavours of the different ingredients. Sweat off the onion and garlic in the oil with the artichokes, add the flour and cook for 2 minutes over a low heat, stirring all the time. Add the vegetable stock, stirring continuously to avoid lumps, and bring to the boil. Add the baby sweetcorn and the chopped cashews and simmer until the sweetcorn is just tender. The cream and sherry are added at the last minute before spooning the mixture into the gougere ring. Decorate with fresh dill and serve.

ASPARAGUS IN FILO WITH A LIME HOLLANDAISE SAUCE

Serves 4

1 bundle thick asparagus spears
4 oz (125g) fromage frais
1 tablespoon fresh dill
1 tablespoon white wine
4 oz (125g) filo pastry
2 oz (50g) melted butter

FOR THE HOLLANDAISE:
4 egg yolks
zest of 1 lime
pinch caster sugar
1 tablespoon white wine vinegar
2 tablespoons fresh lime juice
8 oz (225g) melted butter
salt to taste

Prepare the asparagus and lightly boil or steam for 15 minutes until tender. Discard the tough ends and cut the remaining stalks into 4 inch (10cm) long pieces. Retain the heads (you should have about 12 in all) and finely chop or puree what is left.

Blend the cheese,dill and wine and add the asparagus puree. To assemble, cut the filo into rectangles about 5 inches (12.5cm) wide and brush with butter. Place 3 heads of asparagus at one end, a spoonful of cheese mixture on top and gently roll up, tucking in the ends so you have a neat oblong parcel. Bake in the oven at 400F/200C/Gas 6 for approx. 15 minutes or until golden brown.

To make the hollandaise, whisk together the egg yolks,lime zest and sugar in a double saucepan and gradually add the vinegar and juice until all has been absorbed by the yolks. Continue whisking vigorously whilst trickling in the melted butter. Check for seasoning.

CHOCOLATE CRACKLE
FLAN

Serves 6

FOR THE BASE:
2½ oz (65g) plain chocolate
2´ oz (65g) butter
2 tablespoons golden syrup
1½ oz (30g) caster sugar
2 measures Tia Maria
3½ oz (95g) cornflakes

FOR THE FILLING:
1 banana,1 apple, 1 peach,1 pear,grapes etc
1½ oz (30g) raisins
½ teaspoon lemon juice
brandy to taste
½ pint (275ml) cream,whipped

Melt the chocolate in a basin over boiling water. Add the butter and blend in. Add the golden syrup, caster sugar, Tia Maria and cornflakes, mix well and place on to a greased circular tray. Put into the fridge to set.

Chop the fruit,add the raisins, lemon juice and brandy and fold into the cream. Spread the mixture on to the base and serve.

Shirley Wilkes

THE RIVER HOUSE · LYMPSTONE

This restaurant with rooms is situated on the shores of the River Exe estuary in a picturesque old fishing village which happens to have allotment gardens with the most amazing view down to the English Channel. The sea breezes sometimes turn into gale force winds but we consider this a challenge and still manage to produce the herbs, flowers, fruit and vegetables so necessary for our menu and in particular for our increasing selection of vegetarian dishes.

═══════════

LOVAGE, CHEESE AND ONION TART

Serves 6-8

FOR THE PASTRY CASE:
6 oz (175g) plain flour
pinch salt
3¹⁄₂ oz (100g) butter
3 tablespoons water

FOR THE FILLING:
1 medium-large onion, finely chopped
Cheddar cheese, grated
handful of lovage leaves, finely cut with scissors
10 fl oz (275ml) cream mixed with 3 eggs
salt and freshly ground black pepper
grated nutmeg

Lovage is a wonderfully easy herb to grow. It seems to survive all weathers (except extreme drought) and appears on our allotment/garden year after year ready to flavour soups, casseroles and salads. The leaves are similar to celery but the flavour is quite different – some say it reminds them of walnuts. This is a delicious and unusual savoury beginning to a meal. In the summer we serve it with a skinned, sliced tomato salad, lightly dressed with oil, lemon juice and chopped fresh mint - the combination of the two herbs is superb.

Make the pastry in the usual way and use to make 1 large or individual flan cases. Bake blind in a moderately hot oven and allow to cool before filling.

Cook the onion in butter and oil until soft. Put a layer of onion, then one of grated cheese to cover the bottom of the flan case. Mix the lovage with the cream and egg mixture and the seasonings and pour over the cheese and onion. Bake in a moderately hot oven for about 30 minutes (or 15 minutes for individual tarts) until set.

Cut into slices when cooled a little and garnish with lettuce and landcress leaves.

TERRINE OF CHESTNUT, HAZELNUTS, MUSHROOMS AND CABBAGE WITH LEEK AND POTATO GRATIN

Serves 8

1 bright green loose-leafed cabbage
4 carrots, grated
1 orange
fresh ginger
2 oz (50g) butter
1 tablespoon sunflower oil
1 clove garlic, crushed
4 oz (125g) leeks, sliced
4 oz (125g) mushrooms, diced
2 oz (50g) fresh chestnuts, without shells (if using dried, soak for at least 1 hour first)
2 oz (50g) hazelnuts, toasted in a hot oven to remove skins
2 tablespoons lemon juice
salt and freshly ground black pepper
finely chopped fresh thyme and marjoram
2 eggs

FOR THE SAUCE:
1¹/₂ lbs (700g) tomatoes, chopped (or equivalent of tinned tomatoes)
1 tablespoon tomato purée
1 small onion, chopped
1 red pepper, chopped
2 stalks celery, finely chopped
1 glass medium or sweet white wine
fresh thyme, parsley and marjoram
salt and pepper

FOR THE LEEK AND POTATO GRATIN:
1 small onion, finely chopped
2 oz (25g) butter and 2 tablespoons vegetable oil
1 lb (450g) leeks, finely sliced
1¹/₂-2 lbs (700-900g) potatoes, finely sliced

salt, black pepper and ground nutmeg
white sauce made with 1 oz (25g) butter, 1 oz (25g) flour and 5 fl oz (150ml) milk
¹/₂-³/₄ pint (275-400ml) milk and cream mixed together
finely chopped parsley

Oil an ovenproof terrine dish. Blanch for 2 minutes enough outside cabbage leaves to line the terrine. Blanch the grated carrot for ¹/₂ minute, then cook in a shallow pan over a high heat in 1 oz (25g) butter with the grated zest and juice of the orange and approx. ¹/₂ teaspoon grated fresh ginger. Finely chop the rest of the raw cabbage.

Melt the remaining butter and oil in a shallow pan and gently sweat the leeks, mushrooms, cabbage and crushed garlic until soft. Remove from the heat and add the finely chopped nuts, lemon juice, herbs and seasonings. Lastly add the beaten egg to bind the mixture (you may need a little more or less egg - the mixture needs to be stiff but moist).

Spoon a layer of nut mixture into the terrine lined with cabbage leaves, leaving enough leaf overlapping to be able to fold over the nut mixture. Spoon a layer of carrot mixture over the top, then more nut mixture, then another layer of carrot, finishing with the nut mixture. Fold over the cabbage leaves to completely cover.

Cover with greaseproof paper and foil and bake in a bain-marie in a moderate oven for approx. 1 hour. Allow to cool before turning out and cut into thick slices with a very sharp knife.

Simmer together all the ingredients for the sauce for 1 hour and use to surround the slices of terrine. Because this is rather rich we usually serve it with a crisp green salad, nasturtium flowers when in season, and either a jacket potato with herb butter or a Leek and Potato Gratin made as follows:

Sauté the onion in the oil and butter until soft. Add the leeks and potatoes and turn in the pan to absorb the rest of the butter and mix well with the onion. Season and add the white sauce and enough milk and cream to give a fairly runny mixture. Pour into a shallow gratin dish and bake in a moderate oven for approx. 1 hour, until the potatoes are cooked and have absorbed all the cream and milk. You may need to add a little more cream during cooking time. The finished dish should be brown and bubbling on top. Serve with lots of chopped parsley scattered over.

STRAWBERRY ICED BOMBE

Serves at least 12

FOR THE STRAWBERRY ICE CREAM:
1 lb (450g) fresh or frozen strawberries
1 tablespoon fresh lemon juice
½ pint (275ml) double and ½ pint (275ml) single cream
5 egg whites
10 oz (275g) caster sugar

FOR THE BLACKCURRANT SORBET:
½ lb (225g) blackcurrants
juice of ½ lemon
5 fl oz (150ml) water
4 oz (125g) sugar

You can use almost any fruit in season. In the winter we use dried apricots cooked with orange juice for the ice cream and fresh oranges for the sorbet, or prunes for a contrast of colour. You do not need an ice cream maker or special moulds and it can be made days or even weeks ahead of time.

Make the ice cream and sorbet 2 days before required. Purée the strawberries with the lemon juice in a food processor, then sieve to remove the pips. Whip the creams until thick, then fold in the purée. Whip the egg whites and caster sugar into a thick meringue, fold into the fruit and cream and freeze overnight.

Purée the blackcurrants with the lemon juice, then sieve to remove the pips. Boil the sugar and water for 5 minutes to make a syrup. Mix the fruit juice and syrup together and freeze. When almost set, tip into a bowl and whip well with an electric mixer. Freeze again and when almost set, repeat the whipping process. Freeze.

A day before required, remove the ice cream from the freezer and when soft enough to scoop (20-30 minutes), line a large plastic or metal pudding basin with a thick layer of the ice cream. Fill up with blackcurrant sorbet, then place a layer of ice cream on top to completely hide the sorbet. Freeze.

A few hours before required, dip the bowl containing the bombe into a bowl of hot water (only for a few moments to fractionally melt the ice cream so that it will turn out easily). Put a plate over the top and turn upside down. The bombe should slide out of its bowl on to the plate - if not, repeat the process! Place in the freezer until needed.

Decorate with ribbons and flowers, candles for a birthday or sparklers on New Year's Eve. Definitely a dessert to serve with a flourish for a special occasion!

Robert and Jane Whittington

Lancrigg is situated in one of the most beautiful valleys in the Lake District and serves wholly vegetarian food. The hotel has a relaxing atmosphere with no worry about meat products slipping into the food. Fresh and natural wholefood ingredients are used so as to retain the optimum taste and nutritional value so important to the vegetarian. Most guests are not in fact vegetarian; but judging from the number who come for repeat visits, they are more than happy to try the vegetarian 'alternative'. When we opened our first vegetarian venture in 1980, we invented and adapted from the few vegetarian recipe books available. Now, much more written inspiration is available, but we are great believers in adapting recipes to personal taste and the contents of the store cupboard, with some of the best recipes coming from last minute inspirations!

CHESTNUT AND CELERY SOUP

Serves 4–6

*8 oz (225g) dried chestnuts
1 large onion, chopped
1 large or 2 small heads celery, thoroughly washed and chopped
vegetable oil
2 carrots, washed and chopped
1 tablespoon chopped parsley
2 pints (1.1 litres) vegetable stock
salt and pepper*

I like this soup thick and creamy, but if preferred it can be thinned down with water.

Cook the chestnuts in 2 pints (1.1 litres) boiling water for 2 hours (less cooking time if soaked overnight).

Lightly fry the onion and celery in vegetable oil until the onion is slightly softened. Add the carrots, parsley and vegetable stock. Cover and simmer for 20 minutes. Add the chestnuts together with their cooking liquid. Liquidise thoroughly until smooth and season with salt and pepper.

CARIBBEAN STUFFED PEPPERS WITH SPICED RICE

Serves 4

4 good sized yellow peppers
1 large clove garlic, finely chopped
olive oil or other vegetable oil
1 large onion, chopped
4 sticks celery, chopped
4 oz (125g) creamed coconut, chopped
1 medium sized fresh pineapple, peeled and diced
1 fresh chilli, finely chopped
1 lb (450g) cooked chick peas
salt and pepper
chilli powder (optional)
1 carton soured cream

FOR THE RICE:
1 clove garlic, finely chopped
1 onion, finely sliced
1 tablespoon freshly ground coriander
1 teaspoon freshly crushed cardamom
1/2 teaspoon ground cinnamon
vegetable oil
1 lb (450g) brown basmati rice
4 oz (125g) sweetcorn

FOR THE SAUCE:
1 clove garlic, finely chopped
1 small onion, finely sliced
olive oil
1 small tin tomato purée
juice of 1 lemon
chilli powder
salt and pepper

salad, to accompany (see below)

If you think you've already eaten enough celery in the soup, leave it out, but I like it for its crunchy texture.

Slice the tops off the peppers and deseed them. Place the tops on a greased baking tray and set aside. Put the deseeded peppers upside down on a separate baking tray and roast in a preheated oven (325F/170C/Gas 3) until the skins just begin to wrinkle (about 5-10 minutes). Remove from the oven.

Fry the garlic in the oil and add the onion and celery. Stir in the coconut, pineapple and chilli. Cook, stirring often, until the vegetables are softened but still retain some of their crunchy texture.

Drain the chick peas and roughly mash. Stir into the vegetable mixture and season with salt and pepper. Add a pinch of chilli powder if desired. Fill the peppers with the stuffing mixture and place them upright on the baking tray using some crumpled aluminium foil if necessary to stop them falling over.

Place a good teaspoonful of soured cream on top of each pepper and sprinkle with a pinch of paprika. Pour 1/2 inch (1cm) water around the base of the peppers and set aside while you cook the rice.

For the rice, fry the garlic, onion and spices in the oil, stirring continuously until the onion is translucent. Add the rice and cook for a further 2 minutes, still stirring, then add the sweetcorn. Pour water over the rice, cover and simmer until tender and separate (20-30 minutes). If necessary add more water but do not stir.

Fry the garlic and onion in the oil until starting to change colour. Add the tomato purée and fry for a further 2 minutes on a low heat, stirring continuously. Add 1 pint (570ml) water, the lemon juice and 1/2 teaspoon chilli powder. Stir occasionally and simmer for 5 minutes. Taste and add salt, pepper and more chilli powder if desired.

While the rice is cooking, place the prepared peppers in a preheated oven (325F/170C/Gas 3) for 15-20 minutes. Check occasionally that the water in the baking tin does not dry out. Five minutes before the end of the cooking time, put the pepper tops in the oven.

Spoon some sauce on to a hot plate and place the pepper upright in the middle. Carefully place a pepper lid on to the bubbling soured cream. Serve the spiced rice beside the pepper. Accompany with a salad of crispy green lettuce, watercress, chopped parsley, chopped spring onions and thin slices of fresh pear tossed in olive oil and lemon juice, in a separate bowl.

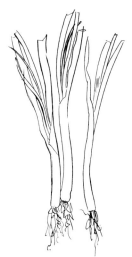

MELON COCKTAIL WITH RASPBERRY AND ELDER-FLOWER SORBET

Serves 4–6

1 ripe water melon (skin should be taut and resonant when tapped with knuckles)
1 honeydew melon (top should be slightly soft when pressed with thumbs)
2 lbs (900g) raspberries, fresh or frozen
4 oz (125g) demerara sugar
5 fl oz (150ml) Hugh Rocks elderflower cordial

This makes a very refreshing end to a delicious dinner! In the season you can make your own elderflower cordial by boiling elderflower heads in sugar and water.

Using a melon baller if available, or a teaspoon, scoop out the melon flesh into a bowl. Cover the bowl and leave to chill thoroughly in the fridge.

Boil the raspberries until soft. Liquidise with the sugar and press through a sieve. Check for sweetness and add more sugar if necessary. Leave the mixture to cool, then add the elderflower cordial and check for taste. Remember that when frozen it will not appear as sweet, so you may need to add more sugar. Place in the freezer, taking out every 45 minutes to beat, then return to the freezer until set.

Serve the melon balls in a glass bowl with a scoop of sorbet.

Alison Yetman

YETMAN'S · HOLT

We opened Yetman's 4 years ago as a small country restaurant housed in a pair of converted cottages. Our daily-changing menu always provides a choice of meat, fish and vegetarian dishes and uses local and organic produce whenever possible. Lots of local fish and shellfish are included on the menu and we like to make full use of wonderful vegetables, fruits and flowers from local gardens; we are self-sufficient for herbs.

MELON, PEAR AND WALNUT SALAD

Serves 4

1 ripe Ogen, Galia or small Honeydew melon
1 ripe Charentais, Rock or small Cantaloupe melon
2 ripe dessert pears
juice of 1 lemon
2-3 oz (50-75g) Stilton, crumbled
8 oz (225g) Greek cow's yoghurt
1 oz (25g) broken walnuts

Quarter and deseed the melons, cut the flesh from the skins and divide into ¾ inch (1.5cm) cubes. Quarter, core and peel the pears, cut each quarter in half lengthwise and sprinkle with lemon juice.

Pile the fruit attractively into bowls and scatter the Stilton on top. Spoon the yoghurt over this and top with the walnuts.

SPINACH, LEEK AND MUSHROOM PÂTÉ BAKED IN PUFF PASTRY

Serves 4

1 lb (450g) flat mushrooms
½ pint (275ml) red wine
1 oz (25g) butter
2 small leeks, trimmed and washed
2 small red peppers, halved and deseeded
1 lb (450g) fresh spinach, washed
salt, freshly ground pepper and nutmeg
1 lb (450g) puff pastry (bought or homemade)
5 fl oz (150ml) cold bechamel sauce
1 egg yolk
crème fraîche or soured cream, to serve

Cut the mushrooms into large dice and put into a shallow-sided pan with the wine and butter. Cook slowly until all the moisture has evaporated and the mixture looks rich and dark. Cool.

Split the leeks down the centre and then across into halves. Plunge into fast-boiling water, return to the boil, drain and refresh under cold running water.

Roast the peppers, skin side up, in the oven on a baking sheet, having first smeared them with a little oil. When they start to bubble and brown a little, the skins should lift away easily. Cool on a plate, then cut into strips.

Blanch the spinach in fast boiling water and refresh. Squeeze dry, chop roughly and season with salt, ground black pepper and nutmeg.

Now assemble the parcels. Roll the pastry into a large rectangle about 14 ins (35.5cm) x 12 ins (30.5cm) and divide into 4 even sized rectangles. Lay 3 or 4 pieces of leek overlapping across the centre of each, then add a layer of spinach, a spoonful of bechamel, then a layer of mushrooms, followed by the strips of pepper and lastly another layer of leek. Fold up the sides of the pastry and form into neat parcels, sealing the edges with a little water. Chill until needed.

Preheat the oven to 425F/220C/Gas 7 and brush the pastry with the egg yolk thinned with a very little water. Gently score a criss-cross of diamonds on the top of each parcel and bake for 30 minutes or until crisp and golden brown. This is good served with a dollop of crème fraîche or sour cream.

PINEAPPLE AND GINGER BOMBE

Serves 8

FOR THE GINGER ICE CREAM:
4 large egg yolks
4 oz (125g) caster sugar
1 heaped teaspoon ground ginger
1 pint (570ml) single cream
6 oz (175g) stem ginger in syrup

FOR THE PINEAPPLE SORBET:
1 small pineapple

¹/₂ pint (275ml) water and 5 oz (150g) granulated sugar, brought to boil, simmered for a few minutes and cooled
juice of 1 lemon
1 small egg white

Whisk the egg yolks and sugar together and sprinkle in the ground ginger. Bring the cream to the boil and pour on to the yolks, whisking thoroughly. Return the mixture to the pan and cook gently, stirring constantly until the custard coats the back of a spoon; don't allow to boil. Strain into a bowl, cover and cool. When cold, stir in the strained ginger syrup and freeze in an ice cream churn. When almost set, finely chop the stem ginger and tip into the ice cream. Churn a little longer to amalgamate and then spoon into a chilled 2¹/₂ pint (1.4 litre) mould or pudding basin.

Have ready a 1¹/₄ pint (700ml) mould or basin, place it centrally on top of the ice cream and gently push down until the ice cream level reaches the top of the outside mould. Drop a weight into the centre mould to prevent it rising while the ice cream freezes. Place in the freezer to set.

Peel, core and dice the pineapple. Liquidise with the syrup and lemon juice. Push through a sieve to remove any fibre, churn in an ice cream maker until slushy, then break up the egg white with a fork and add to the sorbet. Continue to churn until creamy and quite firm.

Remove the ginger ice cream from the freezer and pour warm water into the centre mould to loosen it. Tip the water out, then give the mould a sharp twist one way whilst pulling upwards. The mould should come away cleanly. Spoon the frozen sorbet into the centre and return to the freezer until needed. Remove the bombe from the mould by dipping the outside into warm water. Run a palette knife round the rim and invert on to a plate. The bombe should slide out neatly.

Notes

Notes

Index

Hot Avocado Filled with Cheese and Nuts 46
Leek and Stilton Pancakes 30
Lovage, Cheese and Onion Tart 109
Melon, Pear, Stilton and Walnut Salad 115
Pasta with Mushrooms and Three Cheeses 98
Peaches Stuffed with Cream Cheese 100
Smoked Cheese Roulade 97
Smoked Wensleydale and Spinach Parcels 78
Spinach with Mixed Cheeses 60

CHILLI
Chilli sin Carne with Wild Rice 25
Courgette Fritters with Chilli Sauce 70

CHIVES
Chive Pancakes with Summer Vegetables 53
Cream Cheese and Chive Dip 8
CHESTNUTS
Chestnut and Celery Soup 112
Chestnut and Fig Roll 92
Mille Feuille of Avocado and Chestnut 50
Mushroom and Chestnut Strudel 26
Terrine of Chestnuts and Hazelnuts 110
CHOCOLATE
Chocolate Cheesecake 67
Chocolate Crackle Flan 108
Chocolate Mousse with Cointreau 41
Chocolate Orange Pie 97
Hot Chocolate Fudge Cake 101

Choux Buns with Blue Cheese and Apple 75
Citrus and Walnut Wedge 34

CORIANDER
Butterbean and Coriander Dip 17
jGinger and Coriander Vegetable Crumble 55
COURGETTES
Courgette and Mangetout Strudel 104
Courgette Fritters with Chilli Sauce 70
Courgette Roulade 46
Courgettes with Leeks Ste Foyenne 45

Stuffed Courgettes with Apricots 91

Dutch Potato Soup 68

Eggs au Miroir 77

Fennel and Watercress Soup 55

FILO
Asparagus Filo with Lime Hollandaise 107
Avocado and Brie in Filo Pastry 72
Leek Filo Parcels 57
Spinach and Shiitake Filo Pie 88

Fragrant Palm Hearts 33
Fraises Wilhelmine 103
French Onion Soup 19

FRUIT
Fruity Cashew Cake 13
Oriental Fruit Salad 91
Sour Cream with Dried Fruits 43
Sticky Shortcake Pudding with Preserved Fruits 62
Tropical Fruit Terrine 86

Gaufres de Légumes, Sauce Soubise 102
Gerrard's Sticky Fingers 49

GINGER
Ginger and Coriander Vegetable Crumble 55
Pineapple and Ginger Bombe 116
Sour Cream with Dried Fruits and Ginger 43
Whisky and Ginger Cake 73
HAZELNUTS
Hazelnut Meringue with Brandied Apricots 83
Hazelnut Roast en Croute 17
Terrine of Chestnuts and Hazelnuts 110

HERBS
French Onion Soup with Herb Scones 19
Potato and Fine Herb Soup 30

Hot Chocolate Fudge Cake 101
Hot Passion Fruit Soufflé 51

Iced Saffron, Apricot and Nut Pudding 79
Italian Aubergine and Tofu Layer 85

Julienne of Vegetables Hollandaise 38

Kashmiri Pilaff 10

LEEKS
Courgettes with Leeks Ste Foyenne 45
Leek and Mushroom Cannelloni 14
Leek and Mushroom Croustade 67
Leek and Stilton Pancakes 30
Leek Filo Parcels 57
Spinach, Leek and Mushroom Pâté 115

Lemon Delicious Pudding 25

LENTILS
Lentil and Potato Bake 94
Lentil and Red Wine Soup 26
Lentil and Tomato Lasagne 64
Tarka Dhal 10
LOVAGE
Carrot and Lovage Soup 82
Lovage, Cheese and Onion Tart 109
New Potato Soup with Lovage and Sorrel 52

Mango and Strawberry Trifle 56

MELON
Blueberry and Charente Melon 45
Melon Cocktail 114
Melons and Peaches with Elderflower 54
Melon Gerrard 48
Melon, Pear, Stilton and Walnut Salad 115

Mermaid's Purse 32
Mille Feuille of Avocado and Chestnut 50
Miso and Nori Soup 87

MUSHROOMS
Baked Stuffed Mushrooms 21
Fresh Pasta with Wild Mushrooms 82
Leek and Mushroom Cannelloni 14
Leek and Mushroom Croustade 67
Leek Filo Parcels with Wild Mushroom Sauce 57
Mushroom and Chestnut Strudel 26
Mushroom and Walnut Stroganoff 39
Mushroom and Walnut Strudel 8
Mushroom Soup 80
Pasta with Mushrooms and Three Cheeses 98
Spinach and Shiitake Filo Pie 88
Spinach, Leek and Mushroom Pâté 115

New Potato Soup with Lovage and Sorrel 52

NUTS
Citrus and Walnut Wedge 34
Fruity Cashew Cake 91
Hazelnut Meringue with Brandied Apricots 83
Hazelnut Roast en Croute 17
Hot Avocado filled with Cheese and Nuts 46
Iced Saffron, Apricot and Nut Pudding 79
Melon, Pear, Stilton and Walnut Salad 115
Mille Feuille of Avocado and Chestnut 50
Mushroom and Chestnut Strudel 26
Mushroom and Walnut Strudel 8
Mushroom and Walnut Stroganoff 39
Peaches Stuffed with Cream Cheese and Walnuts 100
Pear and Almond Tart 95
Pistachio Nut Parfait 76
Spinach and Cashew Loaf 22
Sunflower Oatburgers 68
Terrine of Chestnuts and Hazelnuts 110
Toffee Walnut Flan 31

Old Fashioned Bread Pudding 23

ONIONS
Aubergine et Oignons Frits Provencale 103
Cream of Brussel Sprout and Onion Soup 66

French Onion Soup 19
Lovage, Cheese and Onion Tart 109
ORANGES
Carrot and Orange Soup 24
Chocolate Orange Pie 97
Rhubarb, Date and Orange Crumble 65
Tipsy Orange Pancakes 81

Oriental Fruit Salad 91

Parsnip and Apple Soup 98

PASSION FRUIT
Hot Passion Fruit Soufflé 51
Passion Fruit Mousse 9
PASTA
Fresh Pasta with Wild Mushrooms 82
Leek and Mushroom Cannelloni 14
Lentil and Tomato Lasagne 64
Pasta, Pesto and Avocado Salad 84
Pasta with Mushrooms and Three Cheeses 98
Vegetable Ravioli 35
PEACHES
Banana and Peach Vacherin 39
Melons and Peaches with Elderflower 54
Peaches Stuffed with Cream Cheese 100
Peach with Curry Mayonnaise 63

Peacock Pie 12

PEARS
Melon, Pear, Stilton Salad 115
Pear and Almond Tart 95
Pear and Avocado Salad 90

PEPPERS
Caribbean Stuffed Peppers 113
Mushroom Strudel with Red Pepper Sauce 26

Pineapple and Ginger Bombe 116
Pistachio Nut Parfait 76
Piquant Tomato Soup 42

POTATOES
Dutch Potato Soup 68
Lentil and Potato Bake 94
New Potato Soup 52
Potato and Fine Herb Soup 30

Pumpkin Soup 12

Ragout of Black Beans 58
Red Dragon Pie 36
Rhubarb, Date and Orange Crumble 65

RICE
Brochette of Mixed Vegetables with Wild Rice 51
Chilli sin Carne with Wild Rice 25
Kashmiri Pilaff 10

Savoury Bread and Butter Pudding 29
Smoked Cheese Roulade 97
Smoked Wensleydale and Spinach Parcels 78
Sour Cream with Dried Fruits and Ginger 43
Spicy Caribbean Cobbler 40
Spicy Creole Roast 80

SPINACH
Smoked Wensleydale and Spinach Parcels 78
Spinach and Cashew Loaf 22
Spinach and Pine Kernel Pies 29
Spinach and Shiitake Filo Pie 88
Spinach, Leek and Mushroom Pâté 115
Spinach Mousseline 92
Spinach with Mixed Cheeses 60

Sticky Shortcake Pudding 62

STRAWBERRIES
Fraises Wilhelmine 103
Mango and Strawberry Trifle 56
Strawberry and Brandy Brûlé Tart 47
Strawberry Iced Bombe 111

Stuffed Courgettes with Apricots 91
Summer Dream Patissière 89

Sunflower Oatburgers 68
Sweetcorn in a Parmesan Ring 106
Sweet Potato Patties 20

Tarka Dhal 10
Terrine of Chestnuts and Hazelnuts 110
Terrine of Young Vegetables with Pine Kernels 96
Thymes Soup 94
Tipsy Orange Pancakes 81
Toffee Apple Pudding 99
Toffee Walnut Flan 31

TOMATO
Artichoke Hearts with Sundried Tomatoes 44
Lentil and Tomato Lasagne 64
Piquant Tomato Soup 42

Troodos Mountain Pie 61
Two Dips with Crudités 74

Vegetable Crumble 48
Vegetable Harlequin 42
Vegetable Ravioli 35

WALNUTS
Mushroom and Walnut Stroganoff 39
Peaches Stuffed with Cream Cheese and Walnuts
    100
WHISKY
Bread Pudding with Whisky Sauce 37
Whisky and Ginger Cake 73

Yorkshire Curd Tart 20